John Baty's 1839
Groundbreaking Translation of

The Book of Enoch
The Prophet

Including:

His Vigorous Argument that the Book of Enoch
Should be Included in the Bible

Also from SageWorks Press:

The Book of Enoch: Messianic Prophecy Edition
"Time-Capsule to the Last Generation"
by R.I. Burns

and

William Whiston's 1727
Pioneering Translation of Extracts out of
The Book of Enoch

The 21st Century Edition

John Baty's 1839
Groundbreaking Translation of

The Book of Enoch
The Prophet

Including:
His Vigorous Argument that the Book of Enoch
Should be Included in the Bible

R.I. Burns, Editor

SageWorks Press
2023

First KDP print edition, April, 2023 ~ rev. 5/23/23.
San Francisco, CA USA
ISBN: 978-1-68564-450-5
ASIN: 1685644503

Cover Art: Jonathan Bowling

www.TheBookofEnoch.info

*Dedicated to Paul A. Bruce, and
Milton D. Beattie
Who inspired me to rescue from obscurity
John Baty's underappreciated gem*

THE BOOK

OF

ENOCH THE PROPHET.

TRANSLATED FROM THE GERMAN OF ANDREW GOTTLIEB HOFFMANN,

AND CORRECTED OF ITS FORMER MISTAKES,

BY JOHN BATY,

OF ROWELTON IN STAPLETON, CUMBERLAND.

CARLISLE:
SAMUEL JEFFERSON, 34, SCOTCH STREET;

HATCHARD AND SON, PICCADILLY;
AND L. AND G. SEELEY, FLEET STREET, LONDON.

MDCCCXXXIX.

Preface to the 21ˢᵗ Century Edition.

Like the *Book of Enoch* itself, John Baty's 19ᵗʰ century edition of it has been virtually lost. Sad to say, but it seems this little book never did get a very wide reception when it was first published in 1839. From what we can tell, Mr. Baty also seems to have passed on shortly thereafter.

This 21ˢᵗ-century edition seeks to correct this unfortunate situation… This is only proper when we consider John Baty's rendition of the *Book of Enoch the Prophet* has much to recommend it in every way.

The early 19ᵗʰ century was the first time that the complete *Book of Enoch* became available to English readers. John Baty's was only the second English edition. Translators in that era were limited to just the three text copies of the *Book of Enoch* which, in 1773, were brought to the West by explorer James Bruce. About 75 years after Baty's edition, R. H. Charles developed a more eclectic text from which to base his translation since available manuscripts of Enoch by that time had increased in number.

Despite the limited sources, Andrew Gottlieb Hoffmann translated the book into German, which John Baty then translated into English. Both Hoffman and Baty demonstrated a keen ability of knowing when to refer to the available Greek texts to correct textual errors in the Ethiopic. As a shining example of this we have their use of the alternate Greek text for Enoch 2:11 (Charles 7:2).

Here is John Baty's corrected version:

> "And there were born unto them three sorts, the first were great giants, and to the giants were born Nephilim, and to the Nephilim were born Elioud."

In 1821, the RL Laurence version had:

> "And the women conceiving brought forth giants,

whose stature was each three hundred cubits."

That's 450 feet tall! A little later RH Charles will tell us that in fact it is 4500 feet tall or nearly a mile high!

Even after Baty, for the next entire century, *all* translations of the *Book of Enoch* in English opted for the corrupt Ethiopic reading. It would not be until the 21st century that the Nickelsburg/Vanderkam translation would vindicate the Hoffmann/Baty choice by correcting Enoch 2:11 (7:2) in favor of the Greek reading.

Here is the Nickelsburg / Vanderkam translation:

> "And they conceived from them and bore to them great giants. And the giants begot Nephilim, and to the Nephilim were born Elioud."

Besides this commonsense approach to the task of rendering Enoch, John Baty has also presented Enoch's book in a style which is vivid and at times waxing beautiful. The reader is encouraged to read Enoch 15:1-7 (Charles 48), as one example.

In addition, one might argue the Baty version is a worthy addition to anyone's library if for no other reason than the apologetic matter he has included in the front and back of his book. In these additional pages you will read John Baty's ardent protestation and evidence that the *Book of Enoch* should be included as a legitimate part of our body of Scriptures.

This 21st-century edition is offered here in hope of rescuing the Baty version of the *Book of Enoch* from the obscure corners of Biblical investigation and to move it front and center to the attention and the appreciation of believers in Jesus Christ, the Son of Man, to whom the *Book of Enoch* so beautifully bears witness.

R.I. Burns,
Pacifica, California
March 15, 2022

To the reader: *in reprinting Baty's book, effort was made to retain as much as possible of the look and feel for the original volume. Chapter divisions and versification are Baty's original. A key is provided at the back of this edition so the reader can cross-reference any verse in Baty to the more traditional versification system for the Book of Enoch, as was used by R.H. Charles.*

Introduction to the 21st Century Edition.

In late 2017, when we published *The Book of Enoch Messianic Prophecy Edition*, we noted that the *Book of Enoch*, though once thought lost, has been going through a gradual, seemingly unstoppable, process of reemergence on the world scene.

At that time, we noted these stages in this process of reemergence:

- 1773 Rediscovery by James Bruce
- 1821 First English translation by Richard Laurence
- 1883 Revision by Richard Laurence
- 1893 Second major English translation by Robert H. Charles
- 1912 Revision by Robert H. Charles

We now need to revise this accordingly:

- 1839 A vivid new English rendition by John Baty, including his passionate defense of the *Book of Enoch* as a legitimate part of the Bible

In 2006, when I first read the *Book of Enoch*, I noticed on the web there were only a handful of books in print available on this subject. Today, online retailers list many pages of available editions not only of the book itself, but also many books which discuss it.

There are essentially three approaches the authors of these books have been taking in discussing Enoch's book:

The traditional text-critical view:

In this approach, the *Book of Enoch* is regarded as a composite document composed by numerous Jewish writers, between 300 BC to the early first century AD. An example of this perspective would be the Vanderkam/Nickelsburg edition of the *Book of Enoch* and its commentaries. Daniel Olson's translation with commentary also represents this view.

Non-traditional text-critical views:

Individuals with this perspective believe there is something divine about the book, that maybe some parts were written by the Biblical Enoch, but that most of the *Book of Enoch's* final form came together by a number of Jewish writers between 300 BC to early first century AD. Dr. Eugene Scott, J. R. Church and Ken Johnson, are examples of this perspective.

That the book is a legitimate part of the Bible, written by Enoch:

There have been just a handful of individuals who we have found who have taken this view. Ronald K. Brown was probably the first 20th century writer to champion this view. In fact, it was Ronald K. Brown's 1995 edition of the *Book of Enoch* which inspired me in 2006, to begin developing the *Book of Enoch Messianic Prophecy Edition.* However, since that time, I have discovered that over the past three centuries, there have been other occasional champions of the *Book of Enoch.* As far as we now know, William Whiston, friend and colleague of Sir Isaac Newton, was the first English language champion of Enoch's book as early as 1727. However, William Whiston, only possessed a few chapters of Enoch in Greek. Despite this limitation, he had insight and was convinced of its authenticity and published a translation of those fragments and an enthusiastic defense from history for the legitimacy of the *Book of Enoch.*

By 1839, John Baty was fortunate to gain access to the entire *Book of Enoch,* which he translated into English. This was made possible by James Bruce's obtaining three complete copies which he brought back from Ethiopia to Europe.

In this, the 21st century re-publication of John Baty's classic, *The Book of Enoch the Prophet,* the reader will be able to enjoy not only John Baty's translation work, but also his exciting advocacy with evidence for Enoch's inclusion in the Bible! With this edition of Baty's book, we hope to help rescue John

Baty's work from obscurity, bringing it to the attention of a whole new generation of readers.

The *Book of Enoch* is making a comeback in the world in our day, and there are many who believe this is because Enoch's book was intended for our time...

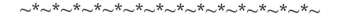

John Baty's *The Book of Enoch the Prophet* **begins here...**

Introduction.

A SHORT ACCOUNT OF THE ALTERATIONS AND CONCEALMENT OF A PART OF THE SCRIPTURES.

The book of Enoch is certainly the most wonderful book in the world, on account of the prophecies which it contains, and other wonderful descriptions of things which are unknown at the present time, of which some require an explanation. But before I attempt to explain them, I earnestly desire the great Almighty Power, the ever-blessed Father, Son, and Holy Spirit, to give me wisdom and understanding, to fill me with the influence of the Holy Spirit, that every thing which I attempt to explain I may explain it right.

The book of Enoch is one of the Hebrew Scriptures which the Jews concealed at Tiberias after the destruction of Jerusalem by the Romans. The Testaments of the twelve sons of Jacob, the Wisdom of Solomon, the Wisdom of the Son of Sirach, and others in the large bibles, and many never discovered were concealed at the same time and place, and from this they received the name of Apocrypha, that is concealed or hidden books. (See Epiphanius Haeres, 30. § 6 and 4).

It may be seen in the Gospel by St. Matthew, chapters xxvi. and xxvii. that the death of our blessed Saviour was caused by the malice of the Jews, and in Chap. xxvii. 63, when our Saviour had foretold his own resurrection, that they did not believe him, and in chapter xxviii. 11, 12, 13, when the watch had declared that our Saviour was risen from the dead, the chief priests gave them money to deny it; and when some of the zealous Christians had shewn that the death and resurrection, and many other particulars concerning our blessed Saviour, had been clearly and distinctly foretold by Enoch, the Jews and Christian heretics corrupted and altered the book of Enoch in many places, particularly in chapters ii. and xxxix. (which are now corrected by the Greek of Syncellus, and the Testament of Levi) and altered the time which Enoch remained on earth in the Bible to bring the book of Enoch into disrepute, and after the destruction of Jerusalem by the Romans, they concealed the book of Enoch, and all others which proved it to be truth, which has been clearly shewn by Epiphanius, Pezron, and Syncellus, and there will more particulars be seen in the notes on chapters ii. and xix. and xxxix. at verse 37. Now the books which were hidden, and concealed, from that received the name of Apocrypha, that is, concealed or hidden books. And they are not on that account to be considered inferior to the rest of the books of the Old Testament, for in some respects the book of Enoch appears to be superior to them all, and the other books are all very useful, but the book of Enoch appears to have been the book to which the Jews had the greatest dislike, because they have rejected all other books of Holy Scripture, which in any degree prove the truth of the book of Enoch, of which I shall give the following brief account.

The Jews concealed the Testaments of the twelve sons of Jacob, because seven of them, viz. Simeon, Levi, Judah, Zebulon, Dan, Naphtali, and Benjamin, have taken quotations from the book of Enoch, and Levi has taken three quotations from it in which there is a prophecy of the life, death, and resurrection of our blessed Saviour by Enoch, (see notes on Chap. xxxix. 37.) And the Jews concealed the books of Esdras, because the second book in chapters ii. 47, and vii. 29, contains prophecies of our Saviour and because the angel Uriel who had shewn many things to Esdras, 2 Esdras iv. 1, &c. is the same angel who explained the revolution of the luminaries to Enoch in chapter xxvii. 1, &c. And the Jews concealed the book of Tobit, because the angel Raphael, who had given instructions to Tobit, and his son, chap. xii. verses 15 to 20, is one of the angels described by Enoch in chapter iii. 1.

And the Jews concealed the Book of Judith, because in her Song, Chap. xvi 7, she mentioned the high giants, the same who are described by Enoch in chapter iv. 13. And the Jews concealed a part of the Book of Esther, because chapter xi. 10, might be compared to the words of our blessed Saviour, John vii. 37, 38, and it might be considered to be a prophecy of our Saviour.

And the Jews concealed the Wisdom of Solomon, because in chapter iv. 10, Solomon had taken this quotation "He pleased God" from the Book of Enoch, chap. xxvi. 19, and because he has in chap. xiv. 6, mentioned the giants, the same described by Enoch chap iv 13. And the Jews concealed the Wisdom of the Son of Sirach, because he has in chapter xliv. 16, taken this quotation "Enoch pleased God" from the Book of Enoch, chap. xxvi. 19, and he has also in chap xvi. 7, mentioned the giants, the same described by Enoch, chap. iv. 13, and he has also in chap. xxiv. 30, described wisdom like to the words of our blessed Saviour, John vii. 37, 38. And the Jews concealed the Book of Baruch, because in chap. iii. 26, he mentions the giants the same described by Enoch chap. iv. 13, and also because he in chap. iii. 34, proves the truth of that part of the Book of Enoch, chap. xxv. 30, in which it is declared that when the names of the stars are called they return an answer. And the song of the three children would be taken out of the Book of Daniel and concealed, because in their song, verses 40, &c. they shew that the sun, moon, and stars, the showers, winds, and dew, &c. all praise before the Almighty, being the same which is shewn by Enoch, chap. xxv. 34, 35, &c., and like all the others this proves the truth of the book of Enoch. And the history of Susanna might be concealed, because the false witnesses against Susanna, ver. 61, had acted like the false witnesses against our blessed Saviour, Mark xiv. 56. And the Jews concealed the books called Maccabees because it is shewn 2 Mac. x. 29, 30, That when the battle waxed hot, there appeared unto the enemies five comely men upon horses with bridles of gold, and two of them led the Jews, and took Maccabeus between them. Now this clearly shews the fulfilment of the prophecy of Enoch in chap. xxxix. 21, 22.

PROOFS OF THE TRUTH OF THE BOOK OF ENOCH.

It has been already mentioned, that seven of the sons of Jacob had taken quotations from the Book of Enoch, but it appears to me that the other five brethren have also taken quotations from it, but they have not mentioned Enoch by name, and the quotations by Solomon, and the son of Sirach have been shewn, but it also appears to be clearly shewn in the note on chapter xv. 23, that what our Saviour called Scripture, could be no other book but the Book of Enoch. And chapter i. 9, of the Book of Enoch has been quoted by St. Jude, verses 14, 15, of his Epistle; and chapter iv. 15, of the Book of Enoch has been quoted both by St. Peter, and St. Jude, see 2 Peter, ii. 4, Jude 6; and chapter xxvi. 19, of the Book of Enoch has been quoted by St. Paul, Hebrews, xi. 5; and it is clear that the words of St. Paul, Heb. ii. 2, refer to the Book of Enoch, chap. ix. 22. And among the fathers of the second century, Tertullian clearly shews that the prophecies of Enoch were from the inspiration of the Holy Spirit. And Irenaeus quoted the Book of Enoch, chap. xxvi. 19, and clearly shews that he knew it to be truth. And Clemens of Alexandria also knew it to be truth. And in Hoffmann's notes it is shewn, that there had been many quotations taken from the Book of Enoch by Origen, and some by Epiphanius, and several by Justyn Martyr who called the giants devils. And the Jews themselves have declared that they have the Book of Enoch, and that it has been carefully preserved from generation to generation, which has been proved by their quotations from it, and this clearly proves the truth of what was said before, that the Jews concealed the Scriptures.

The Book of Enoch was known among Christians until the eighth century of the Christian era, and after that time it appears to have been little known, until the celebrated traveler Bruce brought three copies of it out of Abyssinia. One of these copies was left at Paris; another is among the books of Scripture which he brought home, standing immediately before the book of Job, which is its place in the Abyssinian canon; and a third copy he presented to the Bodleian Library at Oxford, by the hands of Dr.

Douglas, then the bishop of Carlisle. And from this last the learned archbishop of Cashel published an excellent English translation, but it contained the Jewish corruptions, but I have translated this from the German of Andrew Gottlieb Hoffmann, and corrected the Jewish corruptions by a Greek fragment of the book of Enoch in the Chronographia of Georgius Syncellus, or any other way which I found out where I had sufficient authority; and the parts which had been taken away by the Jews or others, I have supplied from the Testaments of Levi and Benjamin, and inserted them in the notes to those places where they had been taken away; and I have got all the principal mistakes corrected; and this translation is published for the purpose of encouraging people to search the Scriptures, that they may be wise unto salvation, that they may make their calling and election sure, and enter into the pleasant and delightful kingdom above, prepared for the righteous by the great Almighty Sovereign. But now I will shew some of the most wonderful of the descriptions given in the Book of Enoch, which have been believed by the writers of the Old and New Testaments, and several of the most wonderful of the prophecies of Enoch concerning our blessed Saviour, which were fulfilled by him, or will be fulfilled at the appointed times, the fulfilment and truth of them being clearly shewn by the writers of the New Testament.

REMARKABLE PLACES IN THE BOOK OF ENOCH PROVED BY SCRIPTURE.

1   Of the coming to judgment, Enoch, i. 9, Jude, 14. 15.

2   The angels took wives, ii. 10, Gen. vi. 2.

3   The commands to bind the evil angels, iv. 6,15, Jude, 6, 2 Peter, ii. 4.

4   The souls of the dead divided, x. 9, 10, Luke, xvi. 26.

5   The souls of the wicked to be punished, x. 12, Luke xvi. 23.

6   Life to be planted in the holy place, x. 29, John xiv. 6.

7   Those before Enoch spoke or prophesied, xii. 1, Luke, i. 70, Acts, iii. 21.

8   Our Saviour shall sit on the throne of his glory, xiv. 3, Mat. xxv. 31.

9   Our Saviour, the Son of man, xiv. 6, Mat. ix. 6.

10   Our Saviour revealed what was concealed, xiv. 7, John, iv. 25.

11   The souls of the dead complained, xiv. 13, Rev. vi. 10.

12   The book of life opened, xiv. 14, Rev. xx. 11.

13   Our Saviour a support for the righteous, xv. 3, John, vi. 41, and xi. 26.

14   The light of nations, xv. 3, John, viii. 12, and ix. 5.

15   The hope of the troubled, xv. 4, Mat. xi. 28.

16   All shall worship him, xv. 4, Phil. ii. 10.

17   He existed before the world, xv. 5, John, i. 1.

18   Believers in him shall be saved, xv. 7, John, iii. 36, Rom. x. 13.

19   The spirits of the righteous are with the Elect One, xv. 14, Luke, xxiii. 43.

20   The earth shall give up the dead, xv. 20, John, v. 28.

21   The righteous shall become angels, xv. 23, Mat. xxii. 30.

22   Our Saviour shall be the judge, xx. 11, John, v. 22.

23   The Son of man was concealed or hid, xxi.10, Rom. xvi. 25.

24   Different degrees of punishment, xxv. 40, Mat. xi. 22, 24.

25   Enoch pleased God, xxvi. 19, Heb. xi. 5, Wisd. iv. 10, Ecclus. xliv. 16.

26   The ten weeks proved beside the chapter, xli.

27   Sin shall not be mentioned in the new heaven, xli. 21, Rev. xxi. 27.

28   The righteous shall shine as the luminaries, xlvii. 2, Mat. xiii. 43.

29   God and his Son will be united with the righteous, xlvii. 13,1 John, i. 3.

30   The righteous shall sit on thrones, xlviii. 25, 26, Rev. i. 6, and iii. 21.

Here I have pointed out thirty places in the Book of Enoch, which are proved by Scripture, and several of them are very remarkable, and clearly shew that they are prophecies of our blessed Saviour or of something remarkable which was to be done, and some of them are such as there are none to be found in the Old Testament, but there are others which are in the Old Testament, but it is not there so particularly shewn that they are prophecies of our blessed Saviour, as it is in the Book of Enoch the righteous. And here are also descriptions of things wonderful, which are proved by Scripture, and they are all proved at the places of the Book of Enoch, which are here pointed out.

And another remarkable proof of the truth of the prophecies of Enoch may be seen in Mat. xxvi. 53, 54, when the chief priests had sent some to take our Saviour, after that St. Peter had drawn his sword, our Saviour said, Thinkest thou that I cannot now pray to my father, and he shall presently give me more than twelve legions of angels. But how then shall the Scriptures be fulfilled, that thus it must be. Now in all the books of the Old Testament, there are no prophecies which clearly shew the life, death, resurrection, and ascension of our blessed Saviour, except the book of Enoch, in which it may be seen Chap. xxxix. 37, and the notes to that verse, that our Saviour is called the Word, John i. 1, and the Word of God, Rev. xix. 13, and in the prophecy of Enoch preserved in the Testament of Benjamin, it is plainly foretold, That the Only begotten of the Highest would be brought into the chief place of judgment, and there the Lord would be insulted, and be raised upon a cross, and the vail of the temple would be rent, and he would arise out of the grave, and ascend from the earth into heaven, and the Spirit of God would go forth upon the nations poured out as fire. Now this clearly shews that the Scriptures spoken of by our Saviour were the Book of Enoch, and others who had copied that prophecy from the Book of Enoch, and that the Book of Enoch was the Book from which all these particular prophecies of our blessed Saviour had been taken, and that as far as we know, there never existed any other such clear prophecies of our blessed Saviour, as those in the Book of Enoch, which clearly shew it to be truth. Also see note on chap. xv. 23.

REMARKS CONCERNING SOME CORREC-
TIONS AND EXPLANATIONS.

The short preface at the beginning was in the manuscript, which Bruce, who brought the Book of Enoch out of Abyssinia, kept to himself.

It may also be observed concerning mount Armon, chap. ii. 7, that the evil angels called that mount, or more properly speaking, the top of that mount, Armon, on which they descended, and on which they swore and as Armon in Hebrew signifies both the top of a mountain, and the residence of a famous chief, it is clearly shewn by Enoch that it was the top of the mount on which the angels swore, and the residence of those famous chiefs before they began their wickedness; and it also appears to be a certain fact, that the land of Armenia received its name from Armen, the third of the leaders of the evil angels, who taught the signs of the earth, and the names of a province or land in Hebrew, which clearly shew the origin of that name, and the land of Armenia is in Hebrew the land of Ararat, and mount Ararat of the Armenians has been clearly shewn to be the mount on which the angels swore, the top of which was called Armon, and the truth of this appears to be clearly shewn by the notes on chap. ii. 7, and the curse of the Almighty upon it is shewn in chap. vii. 16, and the notes. And there were variations in the names of the evil angels which I have not yet shewn. In chap ii. 9, and xxv. 2, and in the Greek of Syncellus it may be seen that there were variations in the following names: The first name Samiaza, was also Amazarak; and the eighth Zakiel, was also Azkeel, and Kael; the tenth Azaziel was also Asael, Azael, Aziel, Azalzel, and Azazel; and the fourteenth Thausael, was also Zavabe; the variation in the first letter might be caused by supposing the Greek Theta, and the Ethiopia Zappa to be the same letter, as they are very like each other; and the fifteenth Samiel was also Samsaveel, and Simapiseel; and the twentieth Sariel was also Araziel and Asaradel.

As the lexicons in Ethiopic are all defective, there is no way of translating some words in the Book of Enoch correctly, but giving the same words used to express the same meaning concerning the same things in Scripture, and that is the way I have done in some places in the Book of Enoch, which before had not been correctly translated; and I can truly say concerning all the alterations which I have made in the Book of Enoch, as far as I know that every thing which I have done is right. Many of them are taken notice of in the notes where the alterations had been made, and shew that they are right, and it may be seen that the rest have been mistakes or Jewish corruptions corrected.

Before I began to translate the Book of Enoch from the German, I earnestly desired the Almighty to give me wisdom and understanding, that every thing which attempted to explain I might explain it right, and certainly what I desired has been given to me, for I was able to translate the Book in very little time, and also to write the notes in little time, and there are many things explained, and many mistakes and Jewish corruptions corrected, which are not to be found either explained or corrected in any other edition of this book, and now I give thanks to the Most High for the wisdom and understanding which he has given me, and say with the Psalmist, O that men would praise the Lord for his goodness, and for his wonderful works to the children of men: Psalm cvii. 8. And I clearly see the truth of the words of the prophet Isaiah, chap xl. 31, But they that wait on the Lord shall renew their strength, and it is certain that I have had more strength than I have had for many years for such a work as I have performed; and the Book of Enoch was translated for the purpose of shewing the great goodness and happiness of those who are truly religious, both in this life, and in that which is to come, and the great misery of those who forget and neglect to perform the commandments of the Most High God; and as this Book contains many remarkable prophecies of our blessed Saviour, and most excellent instructions, it may assist in directing the minds of men to the words of our blessed Saviour, Mat. xxii. 37, 39, Thou shalt love the Lord thy God with all thy heart, and with all thy soul, and with all thy mind, and thou shalt love thy neighbour as thyself. And it may also direct to these words of our Saviour, Mat. vii. 12, Therefore all things whatsoever ye would that men should do to you, do ye even so to them, for this is the law and the prophets. And they who observe these, and other precepts of our blessed Saviour will be happy in this life, and they will obtain everlasting happiness in the life which is to come. And may it be the earnest desire of all people to seek for that happiness, and it they shall certainly obtain, for our blessed Saviour said, John vi. 37, He that cometh to me I will in no wise cast out.

J. B.

CONTENTS, AND PLACES PROVED BY SCRIPTURE.

stars called by their names answer, (see Job xxxii. 35, Baruch iii. 34;)Their conversion into the number of the angels, and of the faithful, (see Dan. xii. 3.)

and sea, and on the sun, moon and stars; 40, Different degrees of punishment, (see Mat. xi. 22, 24.)

Chap. xlviii. 1, Of Noah's birth; 14, The deluge foretold; 22, The dreadful punishments of the wicked; 26, The delightful abodes and everlasting happiness of the righteous; 26, The righteous shall sit on thrones, (proved Rev. i. 6, and iii. 21.)

PLACES IN THE BOOK OF ENOCH PROVED TRUE BY SCRIPTURE.

Enoch i. 8, Rev. xi. 15.

i. 9, Jude, 14, 15.

ii. 2, 10, Gen. vi. 2.

iv. 6, 15, Jude 6, 2 Pe-ter ii. 4.

vi. 23, 1 Tim. vi. 16.

ix. 2, Job xxxviii. 6.

ix. 3, Dan. viii. 8, Rev. vii. 1.

ix. 18, Testament of Reuben.

x. 6, 7, Gen. iv. 10, Heb. xi. 4.

x. 9.10. Luke xvi. 26.

x. 12, Luke xvi. 23.

x. 29, Isaiah xiv. 13.

xii. 15, Rev. vii. 9.

xiii. 3, John viii. 12, and ix. 5. and xii. 46.

xii. 21, Rev. v. 13.

xii. 23, Mat. xxii. 30.

xiii. 1, Rev. vii. 9.

xiii. 23, 2 Peter ii. 4, Jude 6.

xiv. 5, Mat. xxv. 31, Rev. iii. 21.

xiv. 7, Job i. 6, Rev.

xv. 3, Mat. xxv. 31.

xv. 3, John xi. 26.

xv. 4, Mat. xi. 28.

xv. 4. Phil. ii. 10.

xv. 5, John i. 1.

xv. 6, John iv. 25.

xv. 7, Rom. x. 13.

xv. 11, Mat. x. 33.

Enoch xv. 3, John i. I.

xx. 7, Rev. xx. 13.

xx. 7, Mark ix. 46.

xx. 10, Mat. xxv. 31.

xx. 11, John v. 22.

xx. 11, Dan. v. 27.

xx. 14, Rev. v. 13.

xxi. 6, Mat. xii. 36, 37.

xxi. 9, Mat. xxv. 31.

xxi. 10, Rom. xvi. 25.

xxi. 12, Phil. ii. 10.

xxi. 6, Mat. xii. 36, 37.

xxi. 9, Mat. xxv. 31.

xxi. 10, Rom. xvi. 25.

xxi. 12, Phil. ii. 10.

xxi. 17, Rev. vii. 17.

xxii. 15, Mat. vii. 23. xxiii. 15. Rev. xvi. 5.

xxiii. 26, Mat. xii. 36, 37.

xxiii. 30, Rev. xix. 20.

xxv. 15, Wisdom i.13.

xxv. 26, 27, Prov. viii. 29

xxv. 29,30, Job xxxviii. 35, Baruch, iii. 34, Psalm, cxlvii. 4.

xxv. 33, Job xxxviii. 22.

xxv. 34, Psalm cxlviii. 8.

xxv. 38, 39, Mat. xxv. 31

xxv. 40, Mat. xi. 22,24.

xxvi. 13, Rev. iv. 8.

xxvi. 14, Rev. v. 11.

xv. 14, Luke xxiii. 43.
xv. 18, Acts ii. 21.
Enoch xv. 20, John v. 28.
xv. 21, Mat. xxv. 32. xv. 22,
Mat. xix. 28.
xvi. 19, Job xxxviii. 35,
Baruch, iii. 34, Psalm cxlvii. 4.
xvii. 1, Mat. x. 33.
xviii. 3, Rev. xxi. 4. xviii. 5,
Rev. xxi. 25.
xiv. 6, Dan. vii. 9.
xiv. 6, John i. 14.
xiv. 7, John viii. 46.
xiv. 7, John iv. 25.
xiv. 13, Rev. vi. 10.
xiv. 14, Rev. xxi. 11.
xv. I, John vii. 38.

xxvi. 16, Dan. vii. 9.
Enoch xxvi. 19, Heb. xi. 5,
Wisd. iv. 10, Ecclus. xliv. 16.
xxvi. 23, Testament of Levi.
xii. 3, Rev. xxi. 25.
xii. 7, see the notes.
xii. 21, Rev. xxi. 27.
xii. 25, Job. xxxviii. 18.
xliii. 4, Mat. xii. 36.
xliii. 16, Mat. x. 26.
xlvii. 1, Rev. viii. 3, Tobit xii.
15.
xlvii. 2, Mat. xiii. 43.
xlvii. 3, Luke xv. 10.
xlvii. 13, 1 John i. 3, Rev. iii.
20.
xlviii. 25, 26, Rev. i. 6, and iii.
21.

The Book of Enoch.

———

In the name of God, the merciful and gracious, slow to anger, and of great mercy and holiness, this book is the book of Enoch the prophet. May His blessing and help be with him who loves him, for ever and ever, Amen.

CHAP. I.

1 The word of the blessing of Enoch, by which he blessed the elect and the righteous, who were to live in the time of tribulation, to the rejection of all the wicked and ungodly. Enoch a righteous man, who was with God, answered and spoke, when his eyes were open, and he saw a holy vision in the heavens. This the angels shewed me.

2 From them I heard all things, and understood what I saw, that which will not be done in this generation, but in a generation which is to come at a future time, on account of the elect.

3. On their account I spoke and talked with him, who will then go forth from his mansion, the holy and mighty One, the God of this world.

4 Who will then walk upon Mount Sinai, appear with his hosts, and be revealed in the strength of his power from heaven.

5 All shall be afraid, and the watchers shall be terrified.

6 Great fear and trembling shall seize them, even to the ends of the earth, the lofty mountains shall be shaken, and the high hills depressed, and melt like a honey comb in the fire, the earth shall be overflowed, and all which is upon it shall perish, when judgment shall come upon all, even upon the righteous.

7 But to them he will give peace, he will save the elect, and towards them he merciful.

8 So then all shall be made happy and blessed by God, and the splendour of God shall them enlighten.

9 Behold he cometh with ten thousand of his saints, to execute judgment upon them, and to destroy the wicked, and punish all the carnal, for every thing which the sinful and ungodly have done, and committed against him.

10 All who are in the heavens know what there is done.

11 That the lights of heaven change not their paths, that every one rises and sets according to its regulation, every one at its time, without transgression of the divine commands, they see the earth, and understand what there is done, from the beginning of it to the end.

12 That every work of God is unchangeable in the time of its appearance, they behold summer and winter, that the whole earth is full of water, and that it is refreshed by the clouds, the dew, and the rain.

13 They consider and view every tree how it withers, and every leaf falls off, except fourteen trees, which cast not off their leaves, but wait from the old to the new leaf for two or three winters.

14 Again they observe the days of summer, that the sun is direct upon it at their beginning, when you seek for a covered and shady tree, by reason of the burning sun, when the earth is scorched with fervid, heat, and you are neither able to walk upon the ground or upon the rocks, because of that heat.

15 They observe how the trees when they put forth their green leaves, cover themselves, and bear fruit, they understand all, and know that he who lives for ever, does all these things for you.

16 That the works at the beginning of every equal year, that all his works are subservient to him, and unchangeable, yet as God has appointed, so must all things be done.

17   They also behold how the seas and the rivers together perform their labours.

18 But you wait not in patience, nor perform the commands of the Lord, but you oppose and defame his greatness, and the words in your defiled mouths are malignant against his Majesty.

19 Ye withered in heart, for you there shall be no peace.

20 Therefore you shall curse your days, and the years of your lives shall pass away, incessant cursing shall be increased, and you shall obtain no mercy.

21 In those days you shall resign your peace with the eternal maledictions of all the righteous, and sinners shall continually execrate you.

22 They shall execrate you with all the ungodly.

23 The elect shall possess light, joy, and peace, and they shall inherit the earth.

24 But you, ye unholy, shall be accursed.

25 Then wisdom shall be given to the elect, they shall live and shall not again commit offences by wickedness or pride, but they shall humble themselves in the possession of prudence, and shall not repeat offences.

26 They shall not be condemned during the whole time of their lives, nor die in torment and wrath, but the number of their days shall be fulfilled, and they shall grow old in peace, and the years of their happiness shall be increased with joy and with peace, for ever, so long as they shall live.

CHAP. II.

1 It happened after the children of men had increased in those days, that daughters were born unto them elegant and beautiful.

2 And when the angels the sons of heaven saw them, they were inflamed with love of them, and said to each other, Come, let us choose for ourselves wives from the daughters of men, and let us beget children.

3 Then Samiaza their leader said to them, I fear that you may perhaps be averse to the performance of this undertaking,

4 And that I alone shall suffer for so great a crime.

5 But they answered, and said unto him, We all swear:

6 And bind ourselves by mutual execrations, that we will not change our intention, but will perform our intended undertaking.

7 Then they all swore one another, and bound themselves by mutual execrations. Their whole number was two hundred,

who descended in the days of Jared, upon the top of Mount Armon.

8 Therefore they called that mountain Armon, because they had sworn upon it, and bound themselves by mutual execrations.

9 These are the names of their chiefs, the first Samiaza, who was their leader; the second Arstikapha; the third, Armen; the fourth, Akibeel; the fifth, Tamiel; the sixth, Ramiel; the seventh, Danyal; the eight, Zakiel; the ninth, Barakel; the tenth, Azaziel; the eleventh, Armers; the twelvth, Bataryal; the thirteenth, Ananel; the fourteenth, Thausael; the fifteenth, Samiel; the sixteenth, Ertael; the seventeenth, Tumael; the eighteenth, Tarel; the nineteenth, Yomyael; the twentieth, Sariel.

10 These, with all the others, in the thousand one hundred and seventieth year of the world, took to themselves wives, and they continued in their madness with them until the flood.

11 And there were born unto them three sorts, the first were great giants, and to the giants were born Nephilim, and to the Nephilim were born Elioud.

12 And they increased in their power, and taught each other and their wives sorcery and incantations.

13 Moreover, Azaziel taught men to make swords, knives, shields, breastplates, the fabrication of mirrors, the workmanship of bracelets, ornaments, the use of paint, beautifying of the eyebrows, the use of stones of every valuable and select kind, and of all sorts of dyes, so that the world became altered.

14 Impiety increased, fornication multiplied, and they transgressed and corrupted all their ways.

15 Samiaza taught all the sorcerers and dividers of roots.

16 Armers taught the solution of sorcery.

17 Barakel taught the observers of the stars.

18 Akibeel taught signs.

19 Tamiel taught astronomy.

20 Zakiel taught the inspection of the air.

21 Armen taught the signs of the earth.

22 Danyal taught the signs of the sun.

23 And Sariel taught the motions of the moon.

24 And the giants devoured all that the labour of men produced, until it became impossible to feed them, and after that they began to eat the flesh of men, and men began to be few on earth, and they who remained called to heaven concerning that evil, saying, Let a remembrance of us be brought before the Most High.

CHAP. III.

1 And the four great archangels, Michael, Gabriel, Raphael, and Uriel, heard, and from the saints of heaven they looked upon the earth, and saw the quantity of blood which was shed on earth, and all the iniquity which was done upon it, and they said one to another, It is the voice of their cries.

2 The earth bereaved of her children cries even to the gate of heaven.

3 And now, O ye holy ones of heaven, to you the souls of men complain, and say, Procure us justice from the Highest; then they said to their Lord the King, You are Lord of lords, God of gods, King ol kings, the throne of your glory is for ever and ever, and for ever and ever, your name shall be sanctified and glorified, you are praised and glorified.

4 You have made all things, you have power over all things, and all things are open and manifest before you; you see all things, and nothing can he concealed from you.

5 You have seen what Azaziel has done, how he has taught every kind of wickedness upon the earth, and has discovered to the world all the secret things which are done in the heavens.

6 Samiaza also has taught sorcery, to whom you have given power over those who are associated with him, and they have gone together to the daughters of men, have laid with them, and have been defiled.

7 And have disclosed crimes to them.

8 The women likewise have brought forth giants.

9 So the whole earth has been filled with blood, and with wickedness.

10 And now, behold, the souls of those who are dead cry out,

11 And complain even to the gate of heaven.

12 Their groanings ascend, but they cannot escape from the wickedness which is done on the earth. You know all things before they exist.

13 You know these things, and what has been done by them, yet you speak not to us.

14 What in regard to these things ought we to do to them.

CHAP. IV.

1 Then the Most High, the Great and Holy One spoke,

2 And sent Uriel to the son of Lamech,

3 Saying, Go to Noah, and say unto him in my name, Conceal thyself.

4 Then declare unto him an account of the end which is to take place, for the whole earth shall be destroyed, the waters of a flood shall come over the whole earth, and all things which are upon shall be destroyed.

5 And now inform him how he may escape, and how his seed may remain on all the earth.

6 Again the Lord said to Raphael, Bind Azaziel hand and foot, cast him into darkness, open the desert which is in Dudael, and thrust him in there.

7 Throw upon him rugged and pointed stones, and cover him with darkness.

8 There he shall remain for ever, cover his face, that he may not see the light.

9 And in the great day of judgment let him be cast into the fire.

10 Reanimate the earth, which the angels have corrupted, and proclaim life to it, that I may enliven it again.

11 All the sons of men shall not perish in consequence of every secret, by which the watchers have caused destruction, and which they have taught their offspring.

12 All the earth has been corrupted by the operation of the doctrine of Azaziel, therefore ascribe the whole crime to him.

13 Also the Lord said to Gabriel, Go to the giants, the reprobates, the children of whoredom, and destroy the children

of whoredom, the offspring of the watchers from among men; lead them out, and move them one against another, let them perish by slaughter, for they shall not have length of days.

14 They shall all intreat thee, but their fathers shall obtain nothing in regard to them, for they shall hope for eternal life, and that each of them may live five hundred years.

15 Also the Lord said to Michael, Go, and declare his crime to Samiaza, and to the others who are with him who have been united with women, that they might be defiled with all their impurity, and when all their sons shall be slain, when they shall see the destruction of their beloved, bind them for seventy generations in the caverns of the earth, even to the day of judgment and of termination, until the termination of the everlasting judgment.

16 Then they shall be taken to the lowest depths of the fire in torments, and they shall be shut up in prison for ever and ever.

17 Immediately after this he, together with them, shall burn and perish, they shall be bound until many generations shall be fulfilled.

18 Exterminate all the souls devoted to foolishness, and the offspring of the watchers, for they have oppressed mankind.

19 Let all the violent perish from the surface of the earth.

20 Exterminate every evil work.

21 The plant of righteousness and integrity shall appear, and its produce shall become a blessing.

22 Righteousness and integrity shall be planted with rejoicing for evermore.

23 And then all the saints shall give thanks, and live until they have begotten a thousand children, while the whole time of their youth, and their sabbaths shall be finished in peace; and in those days the whole earth shall be cultivated in righteousness, it shall be planted with trees, and filled with blessing, for upon it every tree of delight shall be planted.

24 Upon it vineyards shall be planted, and the vine which shall be planted on it shall bring forth fruit in abundance, every seed which is sown on it shall bring forth for one measure a

thousand, and one measure of olives shall yield ten presses of oil.

25 Purify the earth from all oppression, from all unrighteousness, from all crime, from all ungodliness, and from all the corruption which upon it has been committed, and destroy them from the earth.

26 Then all the children of men shall be righteous, and all nations shall give to me divine honours, and bless me, all shall adore me.

27 The earth shall be purified from all corruption, from all offences, from all pain, and from all suffering, and I will not again send a flood upon it from generation to generation for ever.

28 In those days I will open the treasures of blessing which are in heaven, that I may cause them to descend on the earth, and on all the works and labours of men.

29 Peace and equity shall be associates with the sons of men, all the days of the world in all its generations.

CHAP. V.

1 Before all these things Enoch was concealed, but none of the sons of men knew where he was concealed, where he had been and what had been done.

2 He was entirely employed with the holy ones, and with the watchers in his days.

3 I, Enoch, praised the great Lord and King of peace.

4 And behold the watchers called me Enoch the scribe.

5 Then the Lord said to me, Enoch, scribe of righteousness, go, and declare to the watchers of heaven, who have forsaken the exalted heaven, and their everlasting mansion, and have defiled themselves with women;

6 And have done actions like the sons of men by taking to themselves wives, and they have been greatly polluted on the earth;

7 That on the earth they never shall obtain peace and forgiveness of sin, for they shall not rejoice in their offspring, they shall see the slaughter of their beloved, they shall lament

over the destruction of their sons, and shall solicit for ever, but they shall not obtain mercy and peace.

8 Then I Enoch went on further, and said to Azaziel, Thou shalt not obtain peace, for a great sentence is gone forth against thee, He will bind thee.

9 Neither shall ease, mercy, and intercession be thine, by reason of the oppression which thou hast taught.

10 And by reason of every act of blasphemy, tyranny, and sin, which thou hast disclosed to the children of men.

11 Then I went away, and spake to them all gathered together.

12 And they were all affrighted, and trembled.

13 They besought me to prepare for them a petition, that they might obtain forgiveness, and that I would convey the petition of their prayer before the God of heaven, because they were not able themselves from that time to turn to him, or to lift up their eyes unto heaven, by reason of the ignominious crime for which they had been judged.

14 Then I wrote a petition of their prayer and supplication for their souls, concerning all that they had done, and for the object of their entreaty, that they might obtain forgiveness and rest.

15 Going further, I passed over the waters of Danbadan, which is on the right side of the west of Armon, and read the memorial of their petition until I fell asleep.

16 And behold a dream came to me, and visions appeared above me, I fell down, and saw a vision of punishment, that I might describe it to the sons of heaven, and reprove them. When I awoke, I went to them, they all stood weeping together in Oubelseyael, which is between Libanus and Senezer, with their faces veiled.

17 I related in their presence all the visions which I had seen, and my dream;

18 And began to declare these words of righteousness, and reprove the watchers of heaven.

CHAP. VI.

1 This is the book of the words of righteousness, and of the reproof of the watchers who belong to the world, in consequence of that which He, who is Great and Holy, commanded in the vision. I understood in my dream, that I now spake with a tongue of flesh, and with my breath, which the Almighty has put in the mouth of men, that with it they may speak,

2 And understand with the heart. As He has created and given to men to understand the words of wisdom, so He has created and given to me to reprove the watchers, the offspring of heaven. I have written your petition, and in my vision it has been shewn to me, that what you desire will not be given you, as long as the world remains.

3 Judgment has been passed upon you, nothing will be granted to you.

4 From this time forth you never shall ascend into heaven, He has said that he will bind you on the earth, as long as the world remains.

5 But before these things you shall see the destruction of your beloved sons, you shall not enjoy them, but they shall fall before you by the sword.

6 And ye shall not petition for them, nor for yourselves.

7 But ye shall weep and supplicate in silence. The words of the book which I wrote,

8 A vision that appeared to me;

9 Behold, in that vision, clouds and a mist invited me on, agitated stars and rays of light incited and pressed me forwards, while winds in the vision assisted my flight hastening my going on.

10 They raised me to the height of heaven, I went forward until I came to a wall built with stones of crystal, a moving flame surrounded it, which began to make me afraid,

11 entered into this moving flame;

12 And I came near to an extensive residence, which also was built with stones of crystal, for its walls as well as its floor were stones of crystal, and the ground also was crystal, its roof had the appearance of stars violently agitated, and flashes of lightning, and among them were cherubim of fire, and their heaven was water. A flame burned round its wall, and its portal

flamed with fire. When I entered into this dwelling, it was hot as fire, and cold as ice. No trace of joy or of life was there; fear overcame me and a dreadful trembling seized me.

13 Violently agitated and trembling, I fell on my face. In the vision I saw,

14 And behold there was another far more extensive habitation, to which every entrance before me was open, established in a moving flame.

15 So great was the appearance in every respect, in glory, in magnificence, and in magnitude, that it is impossible to describe to you either its magnificence or extent.

16 Its floor was all on fire, above were lightnings and agitated stars, while its roof displayed a flaming fire.

17 I beheld it attentively, and saw that it contained an elevated throne;

18 The appearance of which was like that of sapphire, while its circumference was like the orb of the radiant sun, and there was the voice of the cherubim.

19 From beneath this mighty throne flowed rivers of flaming fire,

20 To look upon it was impossible.

21 One great in glory sat thereon;

22 Whose robe was brighter than the sun, and whiter than snow:

23 No angel was able to press forward to view the face of Him, the Glorious, and the Effulgent, nor could any mortal behold Him; a fire was flaming around Him.

24 Also a fire of great compass continued to rise up before him, so that none of those who stood around him came near to him, among the myriads of myriads who were before him. To him holy consultation was unnecessary, yet the sanctified, who were near him, departed not far from him either by day or by night, nor were they withdrawn far from him; I also was so far gone forward with a veil before my face and trembling; Then the Lord with his mouth called me, and said, Come near hither, Enoch, at my holy word.

25 And he raised me up, and caused me to come near even to the entrance. My eye was directed to the ground.

CHAP. VII.

1 Then turning himself to me, he spake and said, Hear and fear not, O righteous Enoch, thou scribe of righteousness, draw near hither, and hear my voice, Go say to the watchers of heaven, who have sent thee to pray for them, you ought to pray for men and not men for you.

2 Wherefore have ye forsaken the exalted and holy heaven which remains for ever, and have laid with women, have polluted yourselves with the daughters of men, have taken to yourselves wives, have done like the sons of the earth and begotten a wicked offspring. .

3 Ye who were spiritual, holy, and live a life which is eternal, have defiled yourselves with women, have begotten in carnal blood, have lusted in the blood of men, and have done like those of flesh and blood.

4 These however die and perish.

5 Therefore 1 have given unto them wives, that they might cohabit with them, that sons might be born of them, and that this might be done on earth.

6 But you were made spirits from the beginning, and possess a life which is eternal, and are not subject to death for ever.

7 Therefore I made not wives for you, because ye are spiritual, and your dwelling was in heaven.

8 Now the giants who have been born of spirit and flesh, shall be called evil spirits on earth, and on earth shall be their abode, evil spirits shall come forth from their flesh, because they were created from above, their beginning and original foundation was from the holy watchers they shall be evil spirits on earth, and they shall be called the spirits of the wicked; the habitation of the spirits of heaven shall be in heaven, but terrestrial spirits who are born on earth shall have their habitation on the earth.

9 The spirits of the giants shall be like clouds, which shall oppress, corrupt, fall, quarrel, and wound on earth.

10 They shall cause lamentation, they shall eat no food, and they shall be thirsty, they shall be hidden, and shall not rise up against the sons of men and against women, for they shall come forth during the days of slaughter and destruction.

11 And concerning the death of the giants, the Nephilim, and mighty of the earth, those famous chiefs, wheresoever their spirits may depart from their bodies, let that which in them is fleshly perish before the judgment, and thus they shall perish until the day of the great termination of the great world, for there shall be a destruction of the watchers and the ungodly.

12 And now say to the watchers, who have sent thee to pray for them, who in the beginning were in heaven;

13 In heaven you have been, secret things indeed have not been revealed to you, but you have known a reprobated secret;

14 And this you have related to women in the hardness of your heart, and by that secret, women and men have multiplied evils upon the earth.

15 Say to them, Therefore you never shall obtain peace.

16 And concerning the mount on which they swore, and anathematized themselves by one another, that to the end there shall not depart from it cold, and snow, and frost, and dew, and that which descends upon it shall not descend unless to a curse, until the day of the great judgment, at which time it shall be burned, it shall be made, low, and it shall be burned and melted as wax from the fire, and all the works of it shall be destroyed by fire.

CHAP. VIII.

1 The following are the names of the angels who watch:

2 Uriel, one of the holy angels, who is appointed over alarm and terror.

3 Raphael, one of the holy angels, who is appointed over the souls of men.

4 Raguel, one of the holy angels, who inflicts punishment on the world, and on the luminaries.

5 Michael, one of the holy angels, who is placed over human virtue, rules the nation.

6   Sarakiel, one of the holy angels, who is placed over the souls of the children of men that offend.

7   Gabriel, one Of the holy angels, who is appointed over Ikisat, over Paradise, and over the cherubim; and Phanuel, one of the holy angels, who presides over repentance, and the hope of those who will inherit eternal life.

8   They raised me upon high on a place, where there was the appearance of a burning fire, and when they pleased, they assumed the appearance of men.

9   They carried me to a high place, to a mountain, the top of which reached to heaven.

10   And I saw the receptacles of lightning and of thunder at the end of the place where it was deepest, there was a bow of fire, and arrows in their quiver, a sword of fire, and every sort of lightning.

11 They raised me on high to a splashing stream, and to a fire in the west, which received all the setting of the sun, I came to a river of fire which flowed like water, and emptied itself into the great sea towards the west.

12 I saw every large river until I came to the great darkness, I went to where all flesh go, and I saw the mountains of obscurity which produce winter, and the place from whence the water comes forth in every gulf.

13 I also saw the mouths of all the rivers in the world and the mouths of the deep.

CHAP. IX.

1   I then beheld the receptacles of all the winds, and perceived that in them were the embellishments of the whole creation, and the foundation of the earth.

2   I beheld the stone corners of the earth.

3   I also saw the four winds, which sustain the earth, and the firmament of heaven.

4   And I saw the winds working in the height of heaven,

5   Which arise in the midst of heaven and earth, and compose the pillars of heaven.

6 I saw the winds which turn the sky, which cause the orb of the sun and all the stars to set, and above the earth, I saw the winds which bear up the clouds.

7 I saw the path of the angels.

8 I perceived at the end of the earth, the expanse of heaven above it; then I went on towards the south,

9 Where burnt both by day and night six mountains formed of glorious stones, three towards the east, and three towards the south.

10 Those which were towards the east were of a variegated stone, one of which was like pearl, and another of antimony, and those towards the south were of a red stone, the middle one reached to heaven, like the throne of God, of alabaster, the top of which was of sapphire; I also saw a sparkling fire which was over all the mountains.

11 And there I saw a place on the other side of an extended country, where waters were gathered.

12 I also saw earthly fountains deep in the fiery columns of heaven.

13 And in the columns of heaven I saw fires which descended without number, but not on high, or into the deep, and over these fountains I perceived a place which had neither the expanse of heaven above it, or the solid ground beneath it, neither was the water above it, or aught on the side, but the place was a desert.

14 And there I saw seven stars like great flaming mountains, and like spirits praying to me.

15 Then the angel said, This place will be the prison of the stars, and of the hosts of heaven, until the termination of heaven and earth.

16 The stars which move over fire, are those who transgressed the commandment of the Lord before their time was come, for they came not in the right time, therefore he was angry with them, and bound until the time of the termination of their crimes in the secret year.

17 Then Uriel said, Here the angels who cohabited with women appointed their leaders,

18 And being numerous in appearance caused men to be wicked, and seduced them into errors, so that they sacrificed to devils as to gods, but in the great day there shall be a judgment, with which they shall be judged, until they are destroyed, and their wives also shall be judged, who led astray the angels of heaven that they might salute them.

19 And I, Enoch, I alone saw the likeness of the end of all things, and no human being saw it as I saw it.

20 Then I made a circuit to a place in which nothing was furnished.

21 And there I saw neither the commanding work of a lofty heaven nor of a stedfast earth, but a waste place prepared and terrible.

22 There also I saw in it seven stars of heaven bound together like great mountains, and like a flaming fire: I exclaimed, For what sort of crime have they been bound, and why have they been taken to this place. Then Uriel one of the holy angels who was with me and who conducted me, answered, Enoch, wherefore askest thou, wherefore reasonest thou with thyself, and anxiously searchest out? these are those of the stars who have transgressed the commandment of the most high God, and are here bound until the infinite number of the days of their crime be finished.

23 Afterwards I went further to another terrible place,

24 Where I saw the activity of a great flaming and glittering fire, in the middle of which there was a separation, and fiery columns struggled together to the end of the gulf, and their declivity was deep, but I was not able to discover either its measure or magnitude, and I could not perceive its origin, then I exclaimed, How terrible is this place, and how difficult to search out.

25 Uriel, one of the holy angels who was with me, answered and said, Enoch, why art thou frightened and amazed at this terrible place, at the sight of this place of suffering, he said, This is the prison of the angels, and here they are kept for ever.

CHAP. X.

1 I passed on from there to another place, where I saw on the west a great and high mountain, a strong rock, and four pleasant places.

2 Internally it was deep, spacious, and very smooth, as smooth as it had been rolled over, it was both deep and dark to behold.

3 Then Raphael, one of the holy angels who were with me, answered and said, These are the pleasant places where the spirits, the souls of the dead will be gathered, for them they were prepared, and here will be gathered all the souls of the sons of men.

4 They shall occupy these places in which they dwell until the day of judgment, and until their appointed time.

5 Their appointed time will be long, even until the great judgment. And I saw the spirits of the sons of men who were dead, and their voices reached to heaven while they accused.

6 Then I asked of Raphael, an angel who was with me, and said, Whose spirit is that, the voice of which reaches to heaven and accuses?

7 He answered and said, This is the spirit of Abel, who was slain by Cain his brother, and he will accuse him, until his seed be destroyed from the surface of the earth,

8 Until his seed perish from the seed of the human generation.

9 Therefore at that time I enquired concerning him, and concerning the general judgment, and said, Wherefore is one divided from another? he answered, Three divisions have been made between the souls of the dead, and thus the spirits of the righteous have been divided,

10 Namely, by a gulf, by water, and by light above it;

11 And in the same manner also sinners shall be divided when they die, and shall be buried in the earth, they whom judgment has not overtaken in their lifetime.

12 Here their souls shall be divided, moreover their suffering is great until ths time of the great judgment, the punishment and the torment of those who for ever execrate, whose souls are punished and bound there for ever.

13 And so it has been from the beginning of the world, thus a division has there existed between the souls of those who bring forth complaints, and of those who watch for their destruction, to murder them in the day of sinners.

14 A receptacle of this sort has been made for the souls of ungodly men and of sinners, of those who have committed crimes, and joined with the impious, to whom they are like; but their souls shall not be destroyed in the day of judgment, nor shall they arise from this place. Then I praised God,

15 And said, Praised be my Lord, the Lord of glory and of righteousness, who reigns over all for ever and ever.

16 I went from there to another place towards the west, unto the ends of the earth,

17 Where I saw a fire, flaming and running on without ceasing, which intermitted not its course either by day or by night, but continued always the same.

18 Then I enquired and said, What is this which never ceases?

19 Then answered Raquel, one of the holy angels who was with me,

20 And said, This flaming fire which thou seest running towards the west, is that of all the lights of heaven.

21 I went from there to another place and saw a mountain of fire flaming both by day and night, I went towards it, and beheld seven splendid mountains, which were all different from each other.

22 Their stones were brilliant and beautiful, all were brilliant and splendid to behold, and their surface was beautiful. Three were towards the east, and strengthened by being placed one upon another, and three were towards the south, strengthened in a similar manner, and there were deep valleys, which did not come near one another, and the seventh mountain was in the midst of them. In position they were like the seat of a throne, and odoriferous trees surrounded them.

23 There was among them a tree of an unceasing smell, and there was none of all the sweet cented trees which were in Eden like this in smell; for its leaf, its blossom, and its bark never withered, and its fruit was beautiful,

24 Its fruit was like the clusters of the palm. I exclaimed, Behold, this tree is excellent in appearance, pleasant in its leaf, and the sight of its fruit is delightful to the eye. Then answered Michael, one of the holy and glorious angels who were with me, and who presided over them,

25 And said, Enoch, why enquires thou concerning the odour of this tree?

26 Why art thou desirous to know it?

27 Then I Enoch answered to him, and said, I am desirous of information concerning every thing, but particularly concerning this tree.

28 He answered me and said; That mountain which thou seest, whose head in extension is like the seat of the Lord, will be the seat on which the holy and great Lord of glory, the everlasting King, shall sit when he shall come and descend to visit the earth with goodness.

29 And that tree of a pleasant smell, not one of carnal odour, they shall not be able to touch until the time of the great judgment, when all shall be punished and cast off for ever, this shall be appointed for the righteous and humble, and the fruit of this tree, the tree of life, shall be given to the elect; for towards the north, life shall be planted in the holy place, towards the habitation of the everlasting King.

30 Then they shall greatly rejoice and triumph in the Holy One, the sweet odour shall enter into their bones, and they shall live a long life on earth as thy ancestors have lived; neither in their days shall sorrow, distress, trouble, and punishment afflict them.

31 And I praised the Lord of glory, the everlasting King, because he has made this tree, prepared it for the saints, and declared that he would give it to them.

CHAP. XI.

1 I went from thence to the middle of the earth, and saw a happy and fruitful land, in which branches continually germinated from the trees which were planted there on there I saw a holy mountain, and beneath it water on the eastern side,

which flowed towards the south, I saw also on the east side another mountain as high as that, and there were deep but not wide valleys between them.

2 Water ran towards the mountain to the west of this; and beneath them there was also another mountain.

3 There was a valley but not wide below it, and in the midst of them there were other deep and dry valleys towards the ends of the three, and all these valleys which were deep, but not wide, consisted of a strong rock, and a tree which was planted on them, and I wondered at the rock and valleys, and was much surprised.

4 Then I said, What signifies this blessed land, all these lofty trees, and the accursed valley between them?

5 Then Uriel, one of the holy angels who were with me, answered, This is the accursed valley of the accursed for ever. Here shall be gathered together all who with their mouths have spoken unseemly words against God, and have said disagreeable things of his glory: here they shall be gathered together, here shall be their land.

6 In the latter days, an example shall be made of them in the judgment of righteousness, before the Holy One, while those who have received mercy, shall for ever all their days praise God the everlasting King.

7 And at the time of the judgment they shall praise him for his mercy as he has given it to them. Then I praised God, and turned myself to him, and mentioned his greatness as it was right for me.

8 I went from thence to the east, to the middle of the mountain, in the desert of which I only perceived the level surface.

9 It was full of trees of the seed mentioned, and and water ran down upon it.

10 There appeared a cataract composed as of many cataracts both towards the west, and towards the east; there were trees on one side; on the other, water and dew.

11 Then I went to another mountain from the desert, towards the east of that mountain to which I was near,

12 There I saw trees of judgment, particularly those of the sweet smell of frankincense and myrrh.

13 And over it above them was the elevation of the eastern mountain at small distance.

14 I also saw another place with valleys of water which never diminished,

15 Where I perceived a beautiful tree which in smell was like Mastich.

16 And towards the sides of these valleys I perceived cinnamon of a sweet odour; over them I passed on towards the east.

17 Then I saw another mountain containing trees, from which water flowed like nectar. Its name was Sarira, and Kalboneba, and upon this mountain I saw another mountain upon which were aloe trees.

18 These trees were full like almond trees, and when they brought forth fruit it was superior to all perfume.

19 After these things, I beheld the entrances of the north above the mountains, and perceived seven, mountains filled with pure spikenard, odoriferous trees, cinnamon, and papyrus.

20 From thence I went on above the tops of these mountains to some distance towards the east, and went over the Erythrcean sea, and when I was advanced far beyond it, I went on above the angel Zateel, and came to the garden of righteousness, and in this garden I saw among other trees, some which were numerous and large, and which flourished there.

21 Their fragrance was good and strong, and their appearance was various and beautiful; the tree of knowledge also was there, and if any one eats of it he will obtain more wisdom.

22 It was like a sort of the tamarind tree, and bare fruit like very fine grapes, and its fragrance extended to a considerable distance. I exclaimed, How beautiful is this tree, and how pleasant is its appearance.

23 Then answered Raphael, an angel who was with me, and said, This is the tree of knowledge of which thy ancient father, and thy aged mother ate, who were before thee, and who

received knowledge, when their eyes were opened they saw that they were naked, but they were driven out of the garden.

24   From thence I passed on to the ends of the earth, where I saw large beasts different from each other, and birds different in their appearances and forms, as well as with notes of different sounds.

25 To the east of these beasts I perceived the ends of the earth where heaven ceased, the gates of heaven stood open, and I saw the celestial stars come forth. I numbered them as they came forth out of the gate, and wrote them all down as they came out one after another, according to their numbers, their names altogether, their times, and their years, as the angel Uriel who was with me, had shewn them to me.

26 He shewed them all to me, and wrote them down.

27 He also wrote down for me their names, their regulations, and their operations.

28 From there I passed on towards the north to the ends of the earth;

29 And there I saw a great and glorious wonder at the ends of the whole earth.

30 There I saw heavenly gates opening into heaven, and three of them distinctly divided. The north winds came out from them, and blew cold, hail, frost, snow, dew, and rain.

31 They blew mildly from one of the gates; but when they blew from the other two, it was with force and violence, they blew strongly over the earth.

32 From there I went to the ends of the world towards the west;

33 Where I perceived three gates open as I had seen in the north, the gates and passages through them were of the same extent.

34 Then I went to the ends of the earth towards the south, where I saw three gates open to the south, from which came forth dew, rain, and wind.

35 From there I went to the ends of heaven towards the east, where I saw three heavenly gates open to the east, which had lesser gates within them. Through each of these lesser gates the

stars of heaven passed on, and went towards the west by a path which was seen by them, and that at every time.

36 When I saw them, I praised, every time I praised the Lord of glory, who had made these great and splendid signs, that they might display the magnificence of his works to angels and to the souls of men, that they may glorify all his works and deeds, might see the working of his power, might glorify the great labour of his hands, and praise him for ever.

CHAP. XII.

1 The vision which he saw, the second vision of wisdom, which Enoch saw, the son of Jared, the son of Malaleel, the son of Canan, the son of Enos, the son of Seth, the son of Adam. This is the beginning of the word of wisdom, which I obtained to proclaim and relate to them who dwell on earth. Hear from the beginning, and understand to the end, the holy things which I declare in the presence of the Lord of spirits. Those who were before held it for good to speak.

2 And let not us who come after, hinder the beginning of wisdom, for until the present time, there never has been given before the Lord of spirits, that which I have obtained, wisdom according to the ability of my understanding, and according to the pleasure of the Lord of spirits, that which has been given to me by him, a portion of eternal life.

3 What I received, which was in three parables, I declared to the inhabitants of the world.

4 The first parable: When the assembly of the righteous shall be revealed, and sinners judged for their crimes, and be punished in the sight of the world;

5 When righteousness shall be revealed in the presence of the righteous themselves, who will be chosen for the sake of their good works weighed by the Lord of spirits, and when the light of the righteous and the elect who dwell on earth shall be revealed, where will the habitation of sinners be, and where the place of peace for those who have forsaken the Lord of spirits, it would have been better for them if they never had been born.

6 Also when the secrets of the righteous shall be disclosed, then sinners shall be judged, and ungodly men shall be grieved in the presence of the righteous and the elect.

7 From that time they who possess the earth shall not be mighty and elevated, nor shall they be able to behold the faces of the holy, for the light of the faces of the holy, the righteous, and the elect, has been seen by the Lord of spirits.

8 Yet the mighty kings of that time shall not be destroyed, but shall be given into the hands of the righteous and the holy.

9 And from that time none shall obtain compassion from the Lord of spirits, because their lives in this world will be terminated.

10 In those days the elect and holy generation shall descend from the higher heavens, and their seed shall then be with the sons of men. Enoch received books of indignation and wrath, and books of perplexity and commotion.

11 The wicked shall never obtain mercy, saith the Lord of spirits.

12 A cloud then took me up, and the wind raised me above the surface of the earth, and placed me at the end of the heavens.

13 There I saw another vision, the habitation and resting place of the saints; there my eyes saw their habitation with the angels, and their resting place with the holy ones. They intreated, supplicated, and prayed for the sons of men, while righteousness flowed before them like water, and mercy like dew over the earth, and so it is with them for ever and ever.

14 At that time I saw with my eyes the place of the elect, of faith, truth, and righteousness.

15 The number of the holy and the elect shall be innumerable in the presence of God for ever and ever.

16 I saw their habitation under the wings of the Lord of spirits, all the holy and the elect sung before him, in appearance like a flame of fire, their mouths were full of blessings, and their lips glorified the name of the Lord of spirits, and righteousness continually dwelt before him.

17 There I wished to remain, and my soul longed for that habitation, there was my portion before, for so it was appointed for me by the Lord of spirits.

18 At that time I glorified and exalted the name of the Lord of spirits with blessing and with praise, for he has appointed it with blessing and with praise according to his own will.

19 My eyes a long time beheld that place, I praised and said, Praised be he, praised from the beginning for ever. In the beginning before the world was created, and without end is his knowledge,

20 What is this world? They who sleep not of every existing generation shall praise you, and stand before your glory, praising, glorifying, and exalting you, and saying, The holy, holy, Lord of spirits fills the whole world of spirits.

21 There my eyes saw all who without sleeping stand before him and praise him, and say, Praised be you, and praised be the name of God for ever and ever, then my countenance became altered, until I was unable to see.

CHAP. XIII.

1 After this I saw thousands of thousands, and myriads of myriads, and an infinite number of people stand before the Lord of spirits.

2 On the four wings also of the Lord of spirits on the four sides, I perceived others, besides those who stood before him. Their names also I knew, because the angel who went with me explained them all to me, and discovered to me every secret.

3 Then I heard the voices of those on the four sides praising the Lord of glory.

4 The first voice praised the Lord of spirits for ever and ever.

5 I heard the second voice praising the Elect One, and the elect who suffer for the sake of the Lord of spirits.

6 I heard the third voice petitioning and praying for them who dwell on earth, and supplicate the name of the Lord of spirits.

7 I heard the fourth voice driving out the evil angels, and preventing them from entering into the presence of the Lord of

spirits, to bring forth complaints against the inhabitants of the earth.

8 After this, I desired the angel of peace, who went with me to declare all that was concealed, I said to him, Who are these on the four sides, whom I have seen, and whose words I have heard, and written down? He answered, The first is the merciful, the patient, the holy Michael;

9 The second is he who is over every suffering and every wound of the sons of men, the holy Raphael; the third who is over all that is powerful, is Gabriel; and the fourth, who is over repentance, and the hope of those who will inherit eternal life, is Phanuel. These are the four angels of the most high God, and their four voices which I heard at that time.

10 After this I saw the secrets of the heavens, and of the heavenly kingdom according to its divisions, and of the work of men as they weigh it there in balances; I saw the habitations of the elect, and the habitations of the holy; and then my eyes saw all the sinners who denied the Lord of glory, and whom they were driving out thence, and dragging them away, because punishment was not gone forth against them from the Lord of spirits.

11 There also my eyes saw the secrets of the lightning and the thunder, and the secrets of the winds, how they are divided when they blow over the earth, the secrets of the winds, of the dew, and of the clouds; there I perceived the place from which they came forth, and were filled with the dust of the earth.

12 There I saw the closed receptacles, out of which the winds were divided, the receptacle of hail, the receptacle of snow, the receptacle of the clouds, and the cloud which remained in suspense over the earth before the world.

13 I also saw the receptacles of the moon, from whence they came, whither they run, their glorious return, and how one became more splendid than another, their magnificent course, their unchangeable course, their divided and undiminished course, their observance of a mutual fidelity by a decree to which they adhered, their going forth before the sun, and their attachment to their path in obedience to the command of the Lord of spirits, whose name is powerful for ever and ever.

14 After this, both the concealed and visible path of the moon, as well as the progress of its path was there finished by day and by night, while each, one with another, looking toward the Lord of spirits, exalting and extolling without ceasing, since praise to them is rest; for in the splendid sun there is a frequent changing to blessing and to execration.

15 The course of the path of the moon is light to the righteous, but darkness to sinners, in the name of the Lord of spirits, who created between light and darkness, and divided the spirits of men, and strengthened the spirits of the righteous in the name of his own righteousness.

16 And the angel comes not before this, and he is not endowed with power to come before it, for the judge beholds them all, and judges them all himself in his own presence.

17 Wisdom found no place on earth where she could dwell, therefore her dwelling is in heaven.

18 Wisdom walked forth to dwell among the sons of men, but she received no habitation. Wisdom turned back to her place, and seated herself in the middle of the angels; but wickedness walked forth after her return, who without will found a dwelling, and dwelt among them as rain in the desert, and as dew in a thirsty land.

19 I beheld another splendour, and the stars of heaven. I remarked that he called them all by their individual names, and that they heard. I saw that he weighed out in a righteous balance with their light, the extent of their places, and the day of their appearance and their conversion, splendour brought forth splendour, and their conversion was into the number of the angels and of the faithful.

20 Then I enquired of the angel who went with me, and expounded to me secret things, what they were, he answered, The Lord of spirits has shewn thee a likeness of these, they are the names of the righteous who dwell on earth, and who believe on the name of the Lord of spirits for ever and ever.

21 I also saw another thing in regard to splendour, that it rises out of the stars and becomes splendour, being unable to leave them.

CHAP. XIV.

1 The second parable concerning those who deny the name of the habitation of the holy ones, and the name of the Lord of spirits.

2 They shall not ascend the renewed heaven, and they shall not come on the renewed earth; this shall be the portion of sinners who deny the name of the Lord of spirits, and are thus reserved for the day of punishment and torment.

3 In that day the Elect One shall sit on a throne of glory, and shall appoint their conditions and countless habitations; and when they behold my Elect One, the spirits of those shall be strengthened, who have fled for protection to my holy and glorious name.

4 In that day, I will cause my Elect One to dwell in the midst of them, will renew heaven, will bless it, and enlighten it for ever.

5 I also will renew the earth, will bless it, and will cause those whom I have chosen to dwell upon it, but they who have committed sin and wickedness shall not walk upon it, for I have seen them, I will satisfy my righteous ones with peace, and place them before me, but the condemnation of sinners shall draw near, that I may destroy them from the face of the earth.

6 There I saw the Creator of days, whose head was like white wool, and another was with him, whose face was like that of men, and his countenance was full of grace, like one of the holy angels. Then I enquired of one of the holy angels, who went with me, and who shewed me every secret thing respecting the Son of man, who he was, whence he was, and why he accompanied the Creator of days.

7 He answered and said to me, This is the Son of man, who is righteousness, with whom righteousness has dwelt, and who will reveal all the treasures of that which is concealed, for the Lord of spirits has chosen him, and his portion has conquered all before the Lord of spirits in everlasting righteousness.

8 This Son of man whom thou beholdest shall raise up kings, and the mighty from their couches, and the powerful from

their thrones, shall loosen the bridles of the mighty, and break in pieces the teeth of sinners

9 He shall drive kings from their thrones, and their dominions, because they will not exalt and praise him, nor humble themselves before him, by whom their kingdoms were bestowed upon them, and he will cast down the countenances of the mighty, and fill them with confusion, for their habitation shall be darkness, and their bed worms, and they shall never again expect to be raised from that bed, because they exalted not the name of the Lord of spirits.

10 They shall disdain the stars of heaven, shall lift up their hands against the most High, shall tread upon and inhabit the earth, while they shew forth all their works of wickedness, even all their works of wickedness, and their strength shall be in their riches and their faith in the gods which they have made with their own hands, and they shall deny the name of the Lord of spirits, and shall drive him out of the temples in which they assemble,

11 And with him the faithful who suffer in the name of the Lord of spirits.

12 In that day, the prayer of the holy and righteous, and the blood of the righteous, shall ascend from the earth into the presence of the Lord of spirits.

13 The holy ones who dwell above the heavens shall assemble in that day, and with united voice petition, supplicate, praise, laud, and glorify the name of the Lord of spirits, on account of the blood of the righteous which has been shed, that the prayer of the righteous may not be interrupted before the Lord of spirits, that for their sake he would execute judgment, and that his patience may not endure for ever.

14 At that time, I saw the Creator of days, while he sat upon the throne of his glory, the book of the living was opened in his presence, and all the powers which were in the heavens stood around and before him.

15 Then the hearts of the saints were full of joy, because the accomplishment of righteousness was come, the supplication of the saints heard, and the blood of the righteous esteemed by the Lord of spirits.

CHAP. XV.

1 In that place I saw a fountain of righteousness, which had no scarcity, surrounded by many springs of wisdom, and of these all the thirsty drank, and were filled with wisdom, and had their dwelling with the righteous, the Elect, and the Holy One.

2 In that hour this Son of man was invoked before the Lord of spirits, and his name in the presence of the Creator of days.

3 Before the sun and the signs were created, before the stars of heaven were formed, his name was invoked in the presence of the Lord of spirits. He shall be a support for the righteous and holy to lean upon without falling, and he shall be the light of nations.

4 He shall be the hope of those whose hearts are in trouble. All who dwell on earth shall fall down and worship before him, shall praise and glorify him, and sing hymns of praise to the name of the Lord of spirits.

5 Therefore the Elect and the Concealed One existed in his presence, before the world was created and for ever.

6 And in his presence he has revealed to the saints and to the righteous the wisdom of the Lord of spirits, for he has preserved the lot of the righteous, because they have hated, and forsaken this world of wickedness, and have abhorred all its works and ways in the name of the Lord of spirits.

7 For in his name they shall be saved, and his will shall be their life. In those days the kings of the earth, and the mighty men who have gained the world by the work of their hands, shall be lowly in appearance.

8 For in the day of their anguish and commotion, their souls shall not be saved, and they shall be in the hands of those whom I have chosen.

9 I will cast them like hay into the fire, and like lead into the water, thus they shall burn in the presence of the righteous, and sink in the presence of the holy, and a tenth part of them shall not be found.

10 But in the day of their affliction the world shall obtain repose.

11 They shall fall in his presence, and not be raised up again, for there shall be none to take them out of his hands, and to lift them up for they have denied the Lord of spirits and his Messiah. The name of the Lord of spirits shall be praised.

12 Wisdom is poured forth like water, and glory fails not before him for ever and ever, for he is powerful in all the secrets of righteousness.

13 But wickedness vanishes away like a shadow, and has no fixed station, for the Elect One stands before the Lord of spirits, and his glory is for ever and ever, and his power from generation to generation.

14 With him dwell the spirit of intelligent wisdom, the spirit of understanding and of power, and the spirits of those who sleep in righteousness, and he shall judge secret things.

15 And none shall be able to stand to speak a single word before him, for the Elect One is in the presence of the Lord of spirits, according to his own pleasure.

16 In those days the saints and the chosen shall suffer a change, the light of day shall rest upon them, and the splendour and glory of the saints shall be changed.

17 In the day of tribulation evil shall be heaped upon sinners, but the righteous shall rejoice in the name of the Lord of spirits.

18 It will be shewn to others, that they must repent and forsake the works of their hands, and that honour attends them not in the presence of the Lord of spirits, yet that they may be saved by his name, the Lord of spirits will have compassion on them, for his mercy is great, and righteousness is in his judgment, and in the presence of his glory, and in his judgment unrighteousness shall not stand; he who repents not before him shall perish.

19 Henceforth I will not have mercy on the wicked, saith the Lord of spirits.

20 In those days the earth shall give up from her womb, and the subterranean world give up from hers what it contains, and the abyss shall give again that which it is indebted.

21 He shall separate the righteous and holy from among them, for the day of their redemption has appeared.

22 And in those days the Elect One shall sit upon his throne, while every secret of instructing wisdom shall come forth out of his mouth, for the Lord of spirits has endowed and glorified him.

23 In those days the mountains shall skip like rams, and the hills shall hop like young sheep satisfied with milk, and all the righteous shall become angels in heaven.

24 Their faces shall shine with joy, for in those days the Elect One shall be exalted, the earth shall rejoice, the righteous shall inhabit it, and the elect go and walk upon it.

CHAP. XVI.

1 After that time, in the place where I had seen every secret vision, I was taken up in a whirlwind, and carried towards the west,

2 There my eyes saw the secrets of heaven, and all which was on the earth, a mountain of iron, a mountain of copper, a mountain of silver, a mountain of gold, a mountain of fluid metal, and a mountain of lead.

3 And I enquired of the angel who went with me, and said, What are these things, which in secret I behold?

4 He said, All these things which thou seest shall be for the dominion of the Messiah, that he may reign and be powerful on the earth.

5 And that angel of peace answered me and said, Wait but a short time, and thou shalt see, and every secret thing shall be disclosed to thee which the Lord of spirits hath determined, for these mountains which thou hast seen, the mountain of iron, the mountain of copper, the mountain of silver, the mountain of gold, the mountain of fluid metal, and the mountain of lead, all these in the presence of the Elect One shall be like a honeycomb before the fire, and like water descending from above upon the mountains, and shall become weakened before his feet;

6 In those days they shall not be saved by gold and by silver,

7 And they will not have it in their power to defend themselves and to fly.

8 There shall be neither iron given for arms, nor a coat of mail for the breast.

9 Copper shall be useless, also that shall be useless which neither rusts nor wastes away, and lead shall not be desired.

10 All these things shall be rejected, and perish from the earth, when the Elect One shall appear in the presence of the Lord of spirits.

11 There my eyes saw a deep valley, and its entrance was wide.

12 All who dwell on the land, on the sea, and in islands shall bring to it presents, gifts, and offerings, yet that deep valley shall not be full, their hands shall commit wickedness, for all which they bring forth by labour, the sinners shall devour with crime, but they shall perish from the face of the Lord of spirits and from the surface of his earth, for the righteous shall stand up, and shall not fail for ever and ever.

13 And I saw the angels of punishment, who dwelt there, and prepared every instrument of Satan.

14 Then I enquired of the angel of peace, who went with me, for whom these instruments were prepared,

15 He said they were prepared for the kings and mighty of the earth, that by these they may perish.

16 After this the righteous and chosen house of his congregation shall appear henceforth unchangeable in the name of the Lord of spirits;

17 And these mountains shall not be in his presence as the earth, the hills, and the fountains of water, and the righteous shall be free from the molestation of sinners.

18 Then I looked, and turned myself to another part of the earth, where I saw a deep valley burning with fire.

19 To this valley they brought rulers and the mighty.

20 And there my eyes saw the instruments which they made, fetters of iron in which there was not weight.

21 Then I enquired of the angel of peace who went with me, and said, For whom are these fetters and instruments prepared.

22 He answered, They are prepared for the host of Azaziel, that they may be delivered over and condemned to the lowest

damnation, and that their angels may be overwhelmed with rugged stones, as the Lord of spirits has appointed.

23 Michael and Gabriel, Raphael and Phanuel, shall be strengthened in that day, and shall then cast them into a furnace of flaming fire, that the Lord of spirits may be avenged of them for their crimes, because they became servants of Satan, and deceived those who dwell on earth.

24 In those days punishment shall go forth from the Lord of spirits, and the receptacles which are above the heavens shall be opened, and also the fountains which are under the heavens, and under the earth.

25 All the waters which are in the heavens, and above them shall be mixed together.

26 The water which is above the heaven shall be the agent.

27 And the water which is under the earth shall be the recipient, and all shall be destroyed who dwell upon the earth, and who dwell under the ends of heaven.

28 By this they shall learn to understand the wickedness which they have committed on earth, and by this they shall perish.

CHAP. XVII.

1 Afterwards the Creator of days repented, and said, In vain I have destroyed all the inhabitants of the earth.

2 And he sware by his great name, Henceforth I will not do thus towards all those who dwell on earth.

3 But I will place a sign in the heavens, and it shall be a fidelity between me and them for ever, so long as the days of heaven and earth continue upon the earth.

4 Afterwards, conformable to this my decree, when I shall be disposed to take them unexpectedly by the operation of angels, in the days of affliction and trouble, my wrath and my punishment shall continue upon them, my punishment and my wrath, saith the Lord of spirits.

5 O ye kings, O ye mighty, who inhabit the world, ye shall see my Elect One sitting on the throne of my glory, and he shall judge Azaziel, all his confederates, and all his armies, in the name of the Lord of spirits.

6 There also I saw multitudes of angels, who were moving in punishment, shut up in a network of iron and brass. Then I enquired of the angel of peace, who went with me, To whom those under confine were going,

7 He said, To each of their chosen and their beloved, that they may be cast into the fountains and deep glens of the valley.

8 And that valley shall be filled with their chosen and beloved, the days of whose life shall be terminated, but the days of their failure shall be innumerable.

9 Then princes shall combine together, and conspire. The chiefs of the east among the Parthians and Medes shall dethrone kings, in whom a spirit of amazement shall enter, they shall tumble them from their thrones, springing as lions out of the thickets, and like hungry wolves into the middle of the flock.

10 They shall go up, and tread upon the land of their chosen, which shall be before them, but the threshing floor, the path, and the city of my righteous people shall obstruct their horses, they shall rise up to destroy each other, their right hand shall be strengthened, and a man shall not acknowledge his friend or his brother,

11 Nor the son his father and mother, until the number of the dead bodies shall be full by their death and punishment, and this shall not be done without reason.

12 In those days the mouth of hell shall be opened, into which they shall be thrust, hell shall destroy and swallow up sinners from the face of the elect.

13 After this I saw another army of chariots, which conveyed men,

14 And they came upon the wind from the east, and from the west, and from the south.

15 The sound of the noise of their chariots was heard.

16 And when that agitation began, the saints of heaven perceived it, the pillar of the earth was shaken from its

foundation, and the sound was heard from the ends of the earth unto the ends of heaven at the same time.

17 Then the saints all fell down, and worshipped the Lord of spirits.

18 This is the end of the second parable.

CHAP. XVIII.

1 I now begin to declare the third parable, concerning the righteous and the elect.

2 Happy are ye, O ye righteous and elect, for your lot is glorious.

3 The righteous shall exist in the light of the sun, and the elect in the light of everlasting life, the days of whose life shall never end, and the days of the saints shall not be numbered, who seek for light, and obtain righteousness with the Lord of spirits.

4 Peace be to the righteous with the Lord of the world.

5 Henceforth the saints shall be told that they must seek in heaven for the secrets of righteousness, the portion of faith, for like the sun it has risen upon the earth, and darkness has vanished away, and there shall be light which shall never end, and they shall never attempt to number their days, for before that darkness shall be destroyed, and light will become strong before the Lord of spirits, the light of uprightness will become strong before the Lord of spirits for ever and ever.

6 In those days my eyes beheld the secrets of the lightnings, and the glances, and their judgment.

7 They lighten for a blessing, and an execration, according to the will of the Lord of spirits.

8 And there I saw the secrets of the thunder, when it cracks above in heaven, and its sound is heard.

9 Also the habitations of the earth were shewn to me, the sound of the thunder is for peace, and for blessing, as well as for an execration, according to the word of the Lord of spirits.

10 Afterward every secret of the glances, and of the lightnings was seen by me, for blessing and for fertility they lighten.

11 Then another angel, who went with me spoke to me.

12 And he shewed me the first and last secrets in the height of heaven, and in the depths of the earth.

13 And in the ends and foundations of heaven, and in the receptacles of the winds.

14 He shewed me how their spirits were divided, how they were balanced, and how both the springs and the winds were numbered according to the strength of the spirits.

15 He shewed me the power of the light of the moon, that its power is justice, and the divisions of the stars, their particular names;

16 That every division is divided, that the thunder falls down, that every part which is parted is flash with flash;

17 That their host immediately obey, that the thunder has a resting place, it is endowed with a perseverance in its sound, and the thunder and lightning are not divided, nor move they both with one spirit, yet they are not divided,

18 For when the lightning lightens, the thunder gives a sound, and at its time the spirit rests, and makes an equal division between them, for the provision of their time is as sand, and each of them at its time is restrained with a bridle, and turned by the power of the spirit, which thus propels them according to the abundance of the land of the earth.

19 The spirit of the sea also is powerful and strong, and like a strong power draws it back with a bridle, so it is driven forward, and dispersed against the mountains of the earth. The spirit of the frost has its angel, in the spirit of hail there is a good angel, the spirit of snow on account of its strength has a separate spirit, which ascends from it like vapour, and its name is refrigeration.

20 The spirit of mist is not in union with them in their receptacle, but it has a receptacle by itself, for its mutation is in splendour.

21 In light, and in darkness, in winter, and in summer, its receptacle is bright, and an angel is there.

22 The spirit of dew has its place in the ends of heaven in connection with the receptacle of rain, and its mutation is in winter and in summer, and its cloud and the cloud of the mist are united, one gives to the other, and when the spirit of rain

moves from its receptacle, angels come, and open its receptacle, and bring it forth.

23 When it is scattered over all the earth, it unites at every time with the water on the earth, for the waters are a part which is found on the earth to be nourishment for the earth from the Most High, who is in heaven.

24 Therefore there is a measure in the rain, which the angels receive.

25 I saw all these things, even to the garden of the righteous.

CHAP. XIX.

1 In the five hundredth year, in the seventh month, on the fourteenth day of the month of the lifetime of Enoch, in that parable, I saw that the heaven of heavens shook with a powerful shake, and that the powers of the Most High, and the angels, thousands of thousands, and myriads of myriads, were agitated with a great agitation, and immediately I saw the Creator of days sitting on the throne of his glory, and the angels, and the righteous standing around him. A great trembling came upon me, and terror seized me, my loins were bowed down and relaxed, my whole were loosened, and I fell on my face. The holy Michael, another holy angel, one of the holy ones, was sent to me, and he raised me up.

2 And when he had raised me up, my spirit returned, for I was not able to endure this vision of power, its agitation, and the concussion of heaven.

3 Then holy Michael said to me, Wherefore art thou affrighted at such a vision?

4 This day was the day of mercy, and he has been merciful and forbearing towards all who dwell on the earth.

5 But when the day shall come, and the power, and the punishment, and the judgment, which the Lord of spirits has prepared for those who humble themselves before the judgment of righteousness, for those who deny that judgment of righteousness, and for those who take his name in vain.

6 That day has been prepared for the covenant of the elect, and for the examination of sinners.

7 In that day there shall be distributed two monsters, a female monster, whose name is Leviathan, because it dwells in the depths of the sea above the springs of water.

8 And a male monster whose name is Behemoth, which occupies with his breast the invisible desert;

9 His name was Dendayen in the east of the garden, where the elect and the righteous will dwell, where he received it from my ancestor who was man, from Adam the first of men, whom the Lord of spirits made.

10 And I asked that angel to shew me the power of these monsters, how they became divided on the same day, one being put into the depths of the sea, and one on the earth in the desert.

11 And he said, Son of man, thou here desirest to know what is concealed.

12 And the angel of peace who was with me said to me, These two monsters are by the power of the Almighty prepared to become needful of food, that the punishment of the Almighty may not be in vain.

13 Then children shall be slain with their mothers, and sons with their fathers.

14 And when the punishment of the Lord of spirits rests upon them, so it shall rest upon them, that the punishment of the Lord of spirits may not come upon them in vain. In the end there will be a judgment according to his mercy and forbearance.

CHAP. XX.

1 And I saw in those days that there were long ropes given to those angels, who lifted up their wings and went towards the north.

2 And I enquired of the angel and said, Wherefore have they taken these long ropes and gone forth; he said to me, They are gone forth to measure.

3 The angel who went me said to me, These are measures of the righteous, and the righteous shall bring cords that they may rest upon the name of the Lord of spirits, for ever and ever.

4 The elect shall begin to dwell with the Elect One.

5 And these are the measures which shall be given to faith, and which shall strengthen the word of righteousness.

6 And these measures shall disclose all the secrets in the depth of the earth.

7 And they who have been destroyed in the desert, and they who have been devoured by the fish of the sea, and by wild beasts, shall return, and trust in the day of the Elect One, for none shall perish in the presence of the Lord of spirits, nor shall any be able to perish.

8 Then they altogether kept the commandment above in the heaven; and a power, and a splendour like fire, to them there was given.

9 And first with their voice, they praised him, they exalted him, they glorified him, with wisdom, and displayed wisdom with the word, and with the spirit of life.

10 Then the Lord of spirits placed the Elect One upon the throne of his glory.

11 And he shall judge all the works of the holy above in heaven, and he shall weigh their actions in a balance, and when he shall lift up his countenance to judge their secret ways by the word of the name of the Lord of spirits, and their conduct in the way of the righteous judgment of the great exalted Ruler.

12 They shall together speak with united voice, and bless, glorify, exalt, and praise, in the name of the Lord of spirits.

13 He shall call to every power of the heavens, to all the holy above, and to the power of the Almighty Ruler, the cherubim, the seraphim, and the ophanin, all the angels of power, and all the angels of the Rulers, namely of the Elect One, and of the other Power, who was upon earth over the water on that day,

14 Shall raise their united voice, shall bless, glorify, praise, and exalt, with the spirit of faith, with the spirit of wisdom and patience, with the spirit of mercy, with the spirit of judgment and peace, and with the spirit of benevolence, all shall say with united voice, Praised be he, and praised be the name of the Lord of spirits for ever and ever, praise him all ye who never sleep in heaven above.

15 Praise him all his saints, who are in heaven, and all the elect who dwell in the garden of life, and all the spirits of light, who are able to bless, glorify, exalt, and praise your holy Name, and all of flesh, more than the powers shall glorify and praise your Name for evermore.

16 For the mercy of the Lord of spirits is great, he is longsuffering, and all his works, all his power, by the greatness of his operations, he has revealed to the saints, and to the elect in his own name.

CHAP. XXI.

1 Thus the Lord commanded the kings, the mighty and the elevated, and those who dwell on earth, and said, Open your eyes, and lift up your horns, if ye are able to understand the Elect One.

2 The Lord of spirits sat upon the throne of his glory,

3 And the spirit of righteousness was poured out over him.

4 The word of his mouth shall destroy all the sinners, send all the ungodly, who shall be exterminated by his presence.

5 In that day all the kings, the mighty, and the elevated, and they who possess the earth, shall see and understand that he sits on the throne of his glory, and that the saints shall be judged in righteousness before Him.

6 And that no word which shall be spoken before him shall be in vain.

7 Sorrow shall come upon them as upon a woman in travail, whose labour is hard, when the child comes to the mouth of the womb, and it is made difficult to bring forth.

8 And one portion of them shall look upon another, and they shall be amazed, and shall cast down their countenances,

9 And grief shall seize them, when they shall see this Son of woman sitting on the throne of his glory.

10 Then the kings, the mighty, and all who possess the earth, shall glorify, praise, and exalt him who rules over all things, Him who was concealed, for from the beginning the Son of man was concealed, whom the Highest approved by his power, and revealed him to the elect.

11 He shall sow the congregation of the holy and of the elect, and all the elect shall stand before him on that day.

12 And all the kings, the mighty, and the elevated, and they who rule over the earth shall fell down on their faces before him, and shall worship him.

13 They shall place their hopes on this Son of man, shall implore him, and pray to him for mercy.

14 Then an address shall be given to the Lord of spirits, that they may hasten to expel the wicked from his presence, and their faces shall be full of shame, and shall be covered with darkness, and the angel of punishment shall seize them, that vengeance may be taken on those who have oppressed his children and his elect and they shall become an example to the saints and to his elect, over them these shall rejoice, for the indignation of the Lord of spirits shall rest upon them.

15 Then the sword of the Lord of spirits shall be drunk from them, but the righteous and the elect shall be safe in that day, and from that time they shall not behold the faces of the sinners and the ungodly.

16 The Lord of spirits shall remain over them.

17 And with this Son of man they shall dwell, eat, lie down, and stand up for ever and ever.

18 The righteous and the elect have risen from the earth, and have left off to cast down their countenances, and have been clothed with the garment of life, and that garment of life shall be with the Lord of spirits, and your garment shall not become old, and your glory shall not diminish, in the presence of the Lord of spirits.

CHAP. XXII.

1 In those days the kings and the mighty who possess the earth shall pray to the angels of his punishment, wheresoever they shall be delivered up, that he may give a little rest, and that they may fall down and worship before the Lord of spirits, and confess their sins before him.

2 They shall praise and glorify him the Lord of spirits, and say, Praised be the Lord of spirits, the Lord of kings, the Lord of

the mighty, the Lord of lords, the Lord of glory, and the Lord of wisdom.

3 He shall bring every secret to the light.

4 Your power is from generation to generation, and your glory for ever and ever.

5 Your secrets are deep and numberless, and your righteousness is without measure.

6 We have known that we should glorify and praise the Lord of kings, Him who is King over all kings.

7 And they shall say, Who has given us rest to glorify, laud, praise, and confess in the presence of his glory.

8 And now the rest is short which we desire, but we find it not, we might obtain it, but we lay not hold of it, light has always been wasted before us, and darkness has covered our thrones for ever.

9 For we have not confessed before him, and we have not glorified the name of the Lord of kings, we have not glorified the Lord in all his works, but we have confided in our royalty and our glory.

10 In the day of our tribulation and distress he will not save us, neither shall we find rest. We confess that our Lord is faithful in all his works, in all his judgments, and in his righteousness.

11 He has no regard to persons in his judgments, and we must depart from his presence on account of our evil deeds.

12 And all our sins are truly without number.

13 Then they shall say to themselves, Our souls are satiated with the copiousness of crime;

14 But that prevents us not from descending to the troublesome heat of hell.

15 And hereafter their faces shall be filled with darkness and shame before the Son of man, from whose face they shall be driven away, and before whom the sword shall remain in the midst to expel them.

16 Thus saith the Lord of spirits. This is the decree and the judgment against the mighty, the kings, the elevated, and those who possess the earth in the presence of the Lord of spirits.

17 I also saw other faces in that secret place, I heard the voice of an angel who said, These are the angels who have

descended from heaven to earth, and have discovered secrets to the sons of men, and have seduced the sons of men to commit sin.

CHAP. XXIII.

1 In those days Noah saw that the earth was bent down, and that destruction was near.

2 Then he lifted up his feet from there, and went to the ends of the earth, to the dwelling of his great grandfather Enoch.

3 And Noah cried with a mournful voice, Hear me, hear me, hear me, three times. And he said to him, Tell me what is doing on the earth, for the earth weakens, and is violently shaken; surely I shall perish with it.

4 After this there was a great disturbance on earth, and a voice was heard from heaven, I fell upon my face, when my great-grandfather Enoch came and drew near to me.

5 He said to me, Wherefore criest thou out to me with a mournful cry and lamentation?

6 A commandment has gone forth from the Lord against those who dwell on the earth, that their end may be, for they know every secret of the angels, and every oppression of the devils, and all their secret power, and the power of those who commit sorcery, and the power of binding, and the power of those who pour forth molten images over all the earth.

7 They know how silver is produced from the dust of the earth, and how the drop increases under the earth, for lead and tin are not produced from the earth, as if that were the first fountain from which they are produced.

8 There is an angel stands thereon, and that angel comes forth.

9 Afterwards my great-grandfather Enoch held me with his hand, and said, Go, for I have asked the Lord of spirits concerning this disturbance of the earth; and he said to me on account of their wickedness, innumerable judgments have been consummated before me; they have enquired of me concerning the moons, and they know that the earth with those who dwell

upon it shall perish, and for these there will be no refuge for ever.

10 They have disclosed secrets, and they are those who have been judged, but not thou my son, for the Lord of spirits knows that thou art pure and good, free from the blame of disclosing secrets.

11 He the Holy One has established thy name in the midst of the saints, and will save thee from those who dwell on the earth, and he has established thy seed in righteousness to a king and great glory, and from thy seed shall go forth a spring of righteous and holy men without number for ever.

12 After this he shewed me the angels of punishment, who were ready to come, and to open all the power of waters under the earth.

13 That they may be for judgment, and for the destruction of all those who live together, and dwell upon the earth.

14 And the Lord of spirits commanded those angels who were to go forth, not to take up the men and save them.

15 For these angels were over all the power of water. Then I went away from the presence of Enoch.

16 In those days the voice of the great Ruler came to me, and he said to me, Noah, behold thy portion has ascended up to me, a portion wherein there is no blame, a portion of love, and of justice.

17 And now the angel shall prepare the places shut up, but when they shall proceed to this business, I will put my hand upon it, and save it.

18 The seed of life shall be from this, and a change shall come, that the dry land may not remain empty. I will establish thy seed before me for ever and ever, and the seed of those who shall dwell with thee on the surface of the earth shall never be destroyed from the surface of the earth, and it shall be blessed and multiplied through the earth in the name of the Lord.

19 And they shall confine those angels who disclosed impiety in that burning valley, which at first my great-grandfather Enoch shewed me in the west, where there were mountains of gold, and silver, and iron, and fluid metal, and tin.

20 I saw that valley in which there was great disturbance, and the waters were troubled.

21 And when all this was done, from the flowing of the fire, and the disturbance which troubled them in that place, there was produced a smell of brimstone, which mixed with these waters, and the valley of the angels who seduced others, burned beneath that earth.

22 And rivers of fire flowed through that valley, to which those angels shall be condemned, who seduced the inhabitants of the earth.

23 And in those days the waters shall be to kings, to the mighty, and the elevated, and to the inhabitants of the earth, for the healing of the soul and body, and for the judgment of the spirit.

24 Their spirits shall be filled with sport, that they may be judged in their bodies, because they have denied the Lord of spirits, and they shall see their judgment every day, yet they acknowledge not his name.

25 And as the ardour of their bodies shall be great, there shall be an alteration in their spirits for ever and ever.

26 For no word which is spoken before the Lord of spirits shall be in vain.

27 Judgment shall come upon them, because they trusted in the sport of their bodies, and denied the Lord of spirits.

28 And in those days these waters shall suffer a change, for when the angels shall be judged, in those days the heat of these springs of water will be altered.

29 And when the angels shall ascend, the water of these springs will be changed, and be frozen. Then I heard holy Michael answer and say, This judgment with which the angels shall be judged, is a witness against the kings, the mighty, and those who possess the earth,

30 For these waters of judgment shall be for the healing of the angels, and the death of their bodies, but they shall not see, and not believe, that the waters will be changed, and become a fire, which shall bum for ever.

31 After this he gave me the direction of all the secrets in the book of my great-grandfather Enoch, and in the parables which

had been given to him, and he inserted them for me among the words of the book of parables.

CHAP. XXIV.

1 And on that day, holy Michael answered and said to Raphael, The power of the spirit seizes me, and moves me. The rigour of the judgment, the secret, judgment of the angels, who is able to endure the sharp judgment which is finished and remains? And they were melted by it. Again holy Michael said to holy Raphael, Who is there whose heart is not softened over it, and whose reins are not moved at this voice?

2 Judgment has gone forth against them by those who in such a manner have taken them away, and that was done when they stood before the Lord of spirits.

3 Also holy Rakael said to Raphael, They shall not be before the eye of the Lord, for the Lord of spirits has been angry with them, for they have conducted themselves like lords, therefore a secret judgment shall come upon them for ever and ever.

4 For neither angel or man shall receive a portion of it, but they alone shall receive their own judgment for ever and ever.

CHAP. XXV.

1 After this judgment they shall be put in amazement, and be excited, for it shall be shewn to the inhabitants of the earth.

2 Behold the names of these angels. These are their names. The first of them is Samiaza, the second Arstikapha, the third Armen, the fourth Akibeel, the fifth Tamiel, the sixth Ramiel, the seventh Danyal, the eighth Zakiel, the ninth Barakel, the tenth Azaziel, the eleventh Armers, the twelvth Bataryal, the thirteenth Ananel, the fourteenth Thausael, the fifteenth Samiel, the sixteenth Ertael, the seventeenth Tumael, the eighteenth Tarel, the nineteenth Yomyael, the twentieth Sariel.

3 These are the heads of their angels, and the names of the leaders of their hundreds, and the leaders of their fifties, and the leaders of their tens.

4 The name of the first is Satan: it was he who seduced all the angels the sons of the holy One, and caused them to descend on earth and they corrupted the generation of men.

5 The name of the second is Kesabel, who gave evil counsel to the angels, the sons of the holy One, and seduced them to corrupt their bodies with the generation of men.

6 The name of the third is Gaderel, this is he who discovered every stroke of death to the children of men.

7 He seduced Eve, and shewed the instruments of death to the children of men, the shield, the coat of mail, and the sword for slaughter, every instrument of death to the children of men.

8 From his hand went these to them who dwell on earth from that time and for ever.

9 The name of the fourth is Tenemue, he shewed to the children of men bitterness and sweetness,

10 And shewed them all the secrets of their wisdom,

11 And he taught men to write, and with ink and paper.

12 Therefore they have been numerous who have been mistaken, from every time of the world unto this day.

13 For men were not born for that, with pen and ink to confirm their faith.

14 For they were created to remain righteous and pure like the angels;

15 And death which destroys every thing, would not have been able to hurt them.

16 But by this their knowledge of sin they perish, therefore the power of sin consumes them.

17 The name of the fifth is Kasyade, he shewed to the children of men every wicked stroke of spirits and of demons.

18 The stroke of the embryo in the womb to crush it, the stroke of the spirit by the bite of the serpent, and the stroke which is at noon, the offspring of the serpent, the name of which is Tabaet.

19 This is the number of the Kesbeel, the sum of the decree, which he the Most High, who dwells above in glory, revealed to the holy ones.

20 Its name is Beka. He spoke to holy Michael to shew to them the secret name, that they might see that secret name, and

thus remember the decree, and that they might tremble at that name and decree, they who shewed any secret to the children of men.

21 This is the power of that decree, for it is powerful and strong.

22 And he appointed this decree of Akae by the hands of the holy Michael.

23 These are the secrets of this decree, and by it they were confirmed.

24 Heaven was suspended before the world was created, and for ever.

25 By it the earth has been fixed in suspense over the water, while from the concealed parts of the hills, the clear running waters come forth from the creation of the world, and for ever.

26 By this decree the sea has been formed and its foundation.

27 During the time of its joy he has placed the sand against it, and it is unaltered from the creation of the world, and for ever, and by this decree the abyss has been strengthened, and remains, and it moves not from its place for ever and ever.

28 By this decree the sun and moon fulfil their course, and never depart from their command for ever and ever.

29 By this decree the stars fulfil their courses.

30 And when he calls their names, they answer him for ever and ever.

31 And thus the winds are on the waters, and truly they have spirits, and in their ways a combination of spirits.

32 There the treasures of the sounding thunder are preserved, and the splendour of the lightning.

33 There are preserved the treasures of hail, and of frost, the treasures of snow, and the treasures of rain, and of dew.

34 All these confess and praise before the Lord of spirits.

35 They glorify him with all their power of praise, and he supports them in all that thanksgiving, and they praise, glorify, and exalt the name of the Lord of spirits for ever and ever.

36 And with them he confirms this decree, by which they and their paths are preserved, and their progress never fails.

37 Their joy was great.

38 They praised, glorified, and exalted, because the name of the Son of man was revealed to them.

39 He sat upon the throne of his glory, and the principal part of the judgment was given to him, the Son of man. Sinners shall disappear, and perish from the face of the earth, and those who deceived them shall be bound with chains for ever.

40 According to their degrees of depravity, they shall be imprisoned, and all their works shall disappear from the face of the earth, nor thenceforth shall there be any to corrupt, for the Son of man has been seen sitting on the throne of his glory.

41 Every wicked thing shall disappear, and depart from before his face, and the word of the Son of man shall be confirmed in the presence of the Lord of spirits.

42 This is the third parable of Enoch.

CHAP. XXVI.

1 After this was done, the name of the Son of man living with the Lord of spirits, was exalted by those who dwell on the earth.

2 He was exalted by the chariots of the spirit, and his name went forth in the midst of them.

3 From that day I was not drawn in the midst of them, but he seated me between two spirits, between the north and the west, where the angels received their ropes to measure out a place for the elect and the righteous.

4 There I saw the first fathers, and the righteous who dwell in that place for ever.

5 After this my spirit was concealed, and ascended into the heavens, I saw the angels the sons of the holy One, treading on flaming fire, their garments and raiment were white, and their countenances transparent as crystal.

6 I saw two streams of fire, and the splendour of the fire shone like the hyacinth.

7 And I fell on my face before the Lord of spirits.

8 And the angel Michael, one of the archangels, took me by my right hand, raised me up, and brought me out to where there was every secret of mercy, and secret of righteousness.

9 He shewed me all the hidden things of the ends of the heavens, all the receptacles of the stars, and the splendours of all, from whence they went forth before the face of the holy One.

10 And he concealed the spirit of Enoch in the heaven of heavens.

11 And I saw there in the midst of that light, that there was a mansion built with stones of crystal.

12 And in the midst of these stones were tongues of living fire. My spirit saw an enclosure which enclosed this mansion, and from its four ends came forth streams of living fire, and they encompassed that mansion.

13 And the Cherubim, and Seraphim, and the Ophanin surrounded it, these are they who never sleep, but preserve the throne of his glory.

14 And I saw angels innumerable, thousands of thousands, and myriads of myriads, who surrounded that mansion.

15 Michael, Raphael, Gabriel, Phanuel, and the holy angels who were in the heavens above, went in and out of that mansion. Michael, Raphael, Gabriel and Phanuel, went out of that mansion and holy angels without number.

16 With them was the Creator of days, whose head was white like wool, and pure, and his robe could not be described.

17 Then I fell upon my face, while all my flesh was loosened, and my spirit became changed.

18 I cried out with my voice, with the spirit of power, and I praised, glorified, and exalted.

19 And these praises which went out of my mouth, were pleasing in the presence of the Creator of days.

20 The Creator of days came with Michael, and Gabriel, Raphael and Phanuel, with thousands of thousands, and myriads of myriads of angels without number.

21 And that angel came to me, and with his voice saluted me, and said to me, Thou art the offspring of man, who art born for righteousness, and with thee righteousness remains.

22 The righteousness of the Creator of days shall never forsake thee.

23 He said to me, He shall call to thee Salem by his Name, for the world which exists, for from thence peace has gone forth since the creation of the world.

24 And so he will be with thee for ever and ever.

25 All who exist, and who walk in thy ways of righteousness, shall not forsake thee for ever.

26 Their habitations and their portions shall be with thee, and they shall not be separated from thee for ever and ever.

27 And thus shall length of days be with the Son of man.

28 And there will be peace to the righteous in the direct way of righteousness, in the name of the Lord of spirits for ever and ever.

CHAP. XXVII.

1 The book of the revolutions of the lights of heaven, one according to another as they are, according to their particular divisions, their particular powers, their particular times, their particular names, according to the places of their beginnings, and according to their particular months, which Uriel the holy angel who was with me shewed to me, who is their conductor. The whole account of them he shewed to me according to every year of the world for ever, until a new work shall be formed, which shall be eternal.

2 This is the first law of the luminaries; the sun and the light come by the gates of heaven which are on the east, and on the west are the western gates of heaven.

3 I saw six gates where the sun rises, and six gates where it sets.

4 In these gates also the moon rises and sets, and the conductors of the stars with those who conduct them; six gates were at the rising, and six at the setting of the sun.

5 All these one after another are even, and many windows are on the right, and on the left side of these gates.

6 And first that great light which is called the sun goes forth, the orb of which is as the orb of heaven, and the whole is filled with shining and burning fire.

7 Where its chariot ascends, the wind blows forth.

8 The sun sets in heaven, and turns by the north to go to the east, is conveyed so as to come by that gate, and enlighten the face of heaven.

9 In the same manner it goes forth in the first month by a great gate.

10 It goes through the fourth of these six gates which are at the setting of the sun.

11 And in the fourth gate, through which the sun goes in the first month, there are twelve open windows, from which goes forth a flame, when they are opened at their proper times.

12 When the sun rises in heaven, it goes forth through this fourth gate thirty days, and descends by the fourth gate even with it in the west of heaven.

13 During that time the days lengthened from the day, and the night shortened from the night for thirty mornings long, and then the day is longer by two parts than the night.

14 The day is exactly ten parts, and the night is eight parts.

15 The sun goes fourth through the fourth gate, and sets in it, and turns to the fifth gate, which is in the east during thirty days, after which it goes forth, and sets in the fifth gate.

16 Then the day becomes longer by a second portion, so that it is eleven parts, and the night becomes shorter, and is only seven parts.

17 The sun turns to the east, and comes into the sixth gate, and rises and sets in the sixth gate thirty-one days on account of its signs.

18 At that time the day is longer than the night being twice the night, and becomes twelve parts.

19 But the night is shortened and becomes six parts. Then the sun rises up that the day may be shortened, and the night lengthened.

20 And the sun turns to the east, and comes to the sixth gate, and there it rises and sets for thirty days.

21 When thirty days are expired, the day becomes shortened one part, so that it is eleven parts, and the night is seven parts.

22 Then the sun goes from the west out of that sixth gate, and goes to the east, and goes in at the fifth gate thirty days, and sets again in the west, in the fifth gate of the west.

23 At that time the day becomes shortened two parts, and the day becomes ten parts, and the night eight parts.

24 Then the sun goes forth from the fifth gate, as it sets in the fifth gate, and rises in the fourth gate thirty-one days, on account of its signs, and sets in the west.

25 At that time the day becomes equal with the night, and being equal, the night becomes nine parts, and the day nine parts.

26 Then the sun goes from that gate, as it sets in the west, and turns to the east, and goes forth from the third gate, for thirty days, and sets in the third gate.

27 At that time the night is lengthened from the day during thirty mornings, and the day is shortened from the day during thirty days, the night being exactly ten parts, and the day eight parts.

28 The sun now goes from the third gate, as it sets in the third gate in the west, and turns to the east, and goes forth by the second gate of the east for thirty days.

29 And so it sets m the second gate in the west of heaven.

30 At that time the night is eleven parts, and the day seven parts.

31 And at that time the sun goes from the second gate, as it sets in the second gate in the west, and turns towards the east by the first gate for thirty-one days,

32 And sets in the west in the first gate.

33 At that time the night is lengthened so as to be double the length of the day.

34 It is exactly twelve parts, and the day six parts.

35 The sun has arrived at its elevation, and a second time makes its progress from that elevation.

36 It comes into that gate for thirty days, and sets in the opposite part of heaven in the west.

37 All that time the night is shortened in its length one part, and becomes eleven parts,

38 And the day seven parts.

39 Then the sun turns and comes into the second gate of the east.

40 And it turns by these heights, thirty days rising and setting.

41 At that time the night is shortened in its length, it becomes ten parts, and the day eight parts, then the sun goes from that second gate, and sets in the west, and it turns to the east, and rises in the east in the third gate thirty-one days, and sets in the west of heaven.

42 At that time the night becomes diminished, it is nine parts, and the day is nine parts, and the night is equal with the day. The year is exactly three hundred and sixty-four days.

43 The lengthening of the day and the night, and the shortening of the day and the night, are made to differ from each other by the progress of the sun.

44 By reason of this progress the day is lengthened from the day, and the night shortened from the night.

45 This is the law and progress of the sun, and its turning when it turns back, it turns during sixty days and goes forth. This is the great everlasting light, that which he names the sun for ever and ever.

46 This also is that which goes forth a great light, which is named according to its appearance, as the Lord has commanded.

47 And so it goes in and out without diminishing, or resting, but runs day and night in its chariot, and its light enlightens seven parts from the moon, but the light of both is extended for the same purpose.

CHAP. XXVIII.

1 After this law I saw another law of lesser light, the name of which is the moon, the orb of which is as the orb of heaven.

2 And where its chariot ascends the wind blows forth, and light is given to it by measure.

3 At the beginning and end of every month it is changed, and its days are as the days of the sun, and when in like manner its light is to be, its light is a seventh part from the light of the sun.

4 And when it rises, its beginning is towards the east, it goes forth thirty days.

5 At that time it is seen and is to you the beginning of the month, it is thirty days with the sun in the gate from which the sun goes forth.

6 One half of it being taken away, it is seven portions, and the whole of its orb is without any light, except a seventh portion out of the fourteen portions of its light, in a day it receives a seventh or half that portion of its light. Its light is by sevens, by one portion, and by the half of a portion it sets with the sun.

7 And when the sun rises, the moon rises with it, and receives a half portion of light.

8 And on that night in its beginning in the east, before the day of the month, the moon sets with the sun.

9 And it is dark on that night in its fourteen portions, that is in each half, but it rises on that day with a seventh portion exactly, and it goes forth and turns from the rising of the sun.

10 During the remainder of its time, its light increases to fourteen portions.

11 There I saw another progress and regulation which he made in the law of the moon. The progress of the moons, and every thing relating to them, Uriel the holy angel who conducted them all shewed to me.

12 I wrote down all their situations, as he shewed them to me.

13 I wrote down their months as they are, with the appearance of their light, until it is filled up in fifteen days.

14 In each of its single seven portions, it completes all its light at rising, and in each of its single seven portions, it completes all its darkness at setting.

15 On appointed months it goes its course alone, and in two gates the moon sets with the sun, in the two gates which are in the middle, in the third and fourth gates. It goes forth seven days, and makes its circuit.

16 And it turns again to the gate whence the sun goes forth, and in that makes full all its light, then it declines from the sun, and comes in eight days into the sixth gate, and returns in seven days into the third gate, from which the sun goes forth.

17 When the sun goes forth from the fourth gate, the moon goes forth for seven days, until it goes forth from the fifth gate.

18 Again it turns in seven days to the fourth gate, and there makes full all its light, and turns, and comes by the first gate, eight days,

19 And returns in seven days to the fourth gate, from which the sun goes forth.

20 Thus I saw their situations, according to the fixed order of the months the sun rises and sets.

21 At these times there are in five years, thirty days belonging to the sun. All the days belonging to each year of the five years, when completed, amount to three hundred and sixty-four days, and to the sun and stars belong six days, six days in each of the five years, thus thirty days belong to them.

22 So that the moon has thirty days less than the sun and stars.

23 The moon brings on all the years exactly, that their places may neither be before, or be delayed a single day, but that the exact changing of the year may be in three hundred and sixty-four days. Three years have one thousand and ninety-two days, and five years, one thousand eight hundred and twenty days: so there are in eight years two thousand nine hundred and twelve days.

24 To the moon alone come in three years one thousand and sixty-two days, in five years it has fifty days less than the sun, for an addition being made to the thousand and sixty-two days, in five years there are one thousand seven hundred and seventy days, and the days of the moon in eight years are two thousand eight hundred and thirty-two days.

25 For its days in eight years are less than the days of the sun by eighty days, and these eighty days are what it has less in eight years.

26 The year then becomes truly complete according to the place of the moons, and the place of the sun, which rise in the different gates, which rise and set in them for thirty days.

CHAP. XXIX.

1   These are the heads of the chiefs of thousands, which are over the whole creation, and over all the stars, with the four days which are added, and never separated from their place according to the exact account of the year.

2   And these four days are wanted, which are not reckoned in the account of the year.

3   And men err concerning them, for in truth these lights want, in the place of the course of the world, one day in the first gate, one in the third gate, one in the fourth, and one in the sixth gate.

4   And the course of the world becomes exactly finished every three hundred and sixty-fourth state of it, for the signs;

5   The seasons;

6   The years;

7   And the days Uriel shewed me, the angel whom the Lord of glory, who is for ever, appointed over all the lights of heaven;

8   In heaven, and in the world, that they might rule in the face of the sky, and appear over the earth, and become

9   Conductors of the days and nights, the sun, the moon, the stars, and all the ministers of heaven, who make their revolutions with all the chariots of heaven.

10 Thus Uriel shewed me twelve gates open for the circuit of the chariots of the sun in heaven, from which the rays of the sun go forth.

11 And from these the heat goes forth over the earth, when they are opened at their appointed seasons, they are for the winds, and the spirit of the dew, when in their seasons they are opened at the ends of heavens.

12 I saw twelve gates in heaven at the ends of the earth, through which the sun, moon, and stars, and all the works of heaven go forth at their rising and setting.

13 And many windows are open on their right and on their left side.

14 One window at a certain time grows very hot, so also are those gates from whence the stars go forth, according to their law, and in which they set according to their number.

15 I also saw the chariots of heaven running in the world above, and below these gates in which the stars turns, which

never set. One of these is greater than all, and this goes round the whole world.

CHAP. XXX.

1 And at the ends of the earth I saw twelve gates open for all the winds, from which they come forth, and blow over the earth.

2 Three of them are open in the face of heaven, three in the west, three on the right side of heaven, and three on the left, the first three are those which are towards the east, three are towards the north, three behind those which are on the left towards the north, and three towards the west.

3 From four of these proceed winds of blessing and of health, and from the remaining eight go forth winds of punishment, when they are sent to destroy all the earth, and the water which is upon it, and all who dwell upon it, and all who are in the waters, or on the earth.

4 The first of these winds goes forth from the gate called the eastern, through the first gate on the east, which inclines to the south. From this gate goes forth destruction, drought, heat, and perdition.

5 From the second gate, the middle one, proceeds equity, there come from it rain, fruitfulness, health, and dew; and from the third gate towards the north go forth cold and drought.

6 After these the winds in the direction of the south go forth through three principal gates, through their first gate, which is towards the east goes forth a hot wind.

7 But from the middle gate proceed pleasant odour, dew, rain, health, and life.

8 From the third gate which is towards the west, proceed dew rain, blight, and destruction.

9 After these are the winds towards the north which is called the sea, they proceed from three gates, the first gate is that which is on the east inclining to the south, from this go forth dew, rain, blight, and destruction; from the middle direct gate go forth rain, dew, life, and health; and from the third gate which is

towards the west, inclining towards the north, proceed mist, frost, snow, rain, dew, and blight.

10 After these in the fourth quarter are the winds to the west, and from the first gate inclining to the north, go forth dew, rain, frost, snow, cold, and chill; and from the middle gate go forth dew, rain, health, and blessing.

11 And from the last gate which is southwards, proceed drought, destruction, scorching, and perdition.

12 The account of the twelve gates of the four quarters of heaven is ended.

13 I have shewn all their laws, all their punishment, and all their health, to thee my son Mathusala.

14 The first wind is called the eastern, because it is the first.

15 The second is called the south, because there the Most High descends, and he chiefly there descends, who is praised for ever.

16 The western wind has the name of deficiency, because all the lights of heaven are there diminished, and descend.

17 The fourth wind which is named the north is divided into three parts, one of is them for the habitation of men, another for seas of water, with valleys, woods, rivers, darkness, and snow, and in the third is paradise.

18 I saw seven high mountains higher than all the mountains of the earth, and from them frost goes forth, while days, seasons, and years go on, and pass away.

19 I saw seven rivers upon earth greater than all rivers, of which one comes from the west, and its waters flow into a great sea.

20 Two come from the north to the sea, their waters flowing into the Erythroean sea on the east, and with respect to those which remain, four go forth into the cavity of the north, two to their sea the Erythroean sea, and two are poured into a great sea, where it is said there is a desert.

21 I saw seven great islands on the sea and on the earth, seven in the great sea.

CHAP. XXXI.

1 The names of the sun are these, one Oryares, the other Tomas.

2 The moon has four names, the first is Asonya, the second Ebla, the third Benase, and the fourth Erae.

3 These are the two great lights whose orbs are as the orbs of heaven, and the light of both is extended for the same purpose.

4 In the orb of the sun there is a seventh portion of light, which is given to it from the moon, it is put on by measure, until a seventh part of the light of the sun is departed, they set, and come into the western gate, go round by the north, and by the gate of the east go forth over the face of heaven.

5 When the moon rises, it appears in heaven, and the half of a seventh portion of light is all which is in it.

6 And in fourteen days the whole of its light is completed.

7 By three quintuples light is put into it, until its light is full in fifteen days, according to the signs of the year, it has three quintuples.

8 There will be to the moon the half of a seventh portion.

9 During its diminution on the first day, its light decreases a fourteenth part, on the second day it decreases a thirteenth part, on the third day a twelfth part, on the fourth day an eleventh part, on the fifth day a tenth part, on the sixth day a ninth part, on the seventh day it decreases an eighth part on the eighth day a seventh part, on the ninth day a sixth part, on the tenth day a fifth part, on the eleventh day a fourth part, on the twelfth day a third part, on the thirteenth day a second part, and on the fourteenth day it decreases a half of its seventh part, and on the fifteenth day there is an end of all its light.

10 On fixed months the moon has twenty-nine days.

11 It has also a time of twenty-eight days.

12 Uriel also shewed me another regulation, when light is conveyed into the moon, it is conveyed into it from the sun.

13 All the time that the moon advances with its light, it is conveyed into it from the sun, until in fourteen days its light is completed in heaven,

14 And when it is all finished its light is consumed in heaven, and on the first day it is called the new moon, for on that day it has received light.

15 It becomes exactly full on the day that the sun descends into the west, while the moon ascends from the east in the night.

16 The moon then shines all the night until the sun rises before it, and the moon is seen before the sun.

17 When light comes to the moon, there again it diminishes, until all its light is vanished, and the days of the moon pass away.

18 Then its orb remains empty without light,

19 And in three months it performs its course in thirty days, and in three more months it performs it in twenty-nine days each. These are the times in which it makes its decrease in the first time, and in the first gate, in one hundred and seventy-seven days.

20 And at the time of its going forth during three months it appears thirty days each, and during three months it appears twenty-nine days.

21 For each twenty days it appears in the night as a man, and in the day as heaven, for there is nothing in it except its' light.

CHAP. XXXII.

1 And now my son Mathusala, I have shewn thee every thing, and the account of every ordinance of the stars of heaven is ended.

2 Uriel shewed me all their ordinances, which are on all days, and in every time, which are under every power, and in every year, at its egression, according to its law, in every month, and in every week, and the decrease of the moon, which is effected in the sixth gate, for in that gate its light is ended.

3 The beginning of the month is from this, and its decrease which is effected in the sixth gate in its time to the end are one hundred and seventy seven days, according to its ordinance by twenty-five weeks, and two days.

4 And its time is less than that of the sun according to the ordinance of the stars by five days in one half year exactly, when they are at the end of that, situation which thou seest.

5 Such is the appearance and likeness of every light, which Uriel shewed to me, the great angel who is their conductor.

6 In those days Uriel answered and said to me, Behold, O Enoch, I have shewed thee all things,

7 And I have revealed all things to thee. Thou seest the sun, and the moon, and those which conduct the stars of heaven, and all those which cause all their operations, times, and egressions.

8 In the days of sinners the years shall be shortened.

9 Their seed shall be backward on the earth, and on their pasturage, and every thing done on earth shall be turned back, and not appear in its time, the rain shall be kept back, and heaven shall stand still.

10 In those days the fruits of the earth shall be late, and not germinate in their time, and the fruits of the earth shall be kept back in that time.

11 The moon shall change its laws, and not be seen at its time, but in those days heaven shall be seen, and unfruitfulness shall take place in the frontiers of the great chariots in the west, and he shall shine more than the orders of lights, and many heads among the stars of power shall err, perverting their ways and works.

12 They shall not appear in their season who command them, and all the orders of the stars shall be shut up against sinners.

13 The thoughts of those who dwell on earth shall transgress within them, and they shall be perverted in all their ways.

14 They shall transgress and hold themselves to be gods, while misery shall be great among them,

15 And punishment shall come upon them, so that they all shall be destroyed.

16 He said to me, O Enoch, look on the book which heaven has dropped down, and read that which is written therein, and understand every part.

17 Then I looked on that which dropped from heaven, and read all that was written, and understood all, and read the book, and all which was written therein, and all the works of men,

18 And of all the children of flesh upon earth during the regeneration of the world.

19 Immediately after I praised the Lord, the King of glory, who has thus made the whole work of the world.

20 And I glorified the Lord, on account of his patience and blessing towards the children of the world.

21 I said at that time, Blessed is the man who shall die righteous and good, against whom a record of wickedness has not been written, and with whom a crime is not found.

22 Then these three holy ones brought me near, and set me on the earth before the door of my house.

23 And they said unto me, Explain every thing to Mathusala thy son, and inform all thy children that what is flesh shall not be justified before the Lord, for he is their Creator.

24 We will leave thee for one year with thy children, until thou again art strong, that thou mayest teach thy children, write for them, and explain all to thy children; but in another year they will take thee from the midst of them, and thy heart shall be strengthened, for the good shall declare righteousness to the good, the righteous shall rejoice with the righteous, and profess among one another, but sinners with sinners shall die.

25 And the perverted with the perverted shall be drowned.

26 And those who act righteously shall die by reason of the works of men, and shall be gathered together by reason of the works of the ungodly.

27 In those days they ceased to converse with me.

28 And I came to my fellow men, while I praised the Lord of worlds.

CHAP. XXXIII.

1 Now my son Mathusala, all these things I speak unto thee, and write for thee; I have revealed all to thee, and have given thee books of every thing.

2 My son Mathusala, preserve thou the books received from the hand of thy father, that thou mayest give them to the generations of the world.

3 I have given wisdom to thee, and to thy children and to those who shall proceed from their children, that this wisdom may be in the thoughts of their children, and in the thoughts of the generation of generations for ever, and that those who understand it may not slumber, but ear with their ears, that they may learn this wisdom, and that they may be thought worthy of eating this wholesome food, which shall be eaten by the righteous.

4 Blessed are all the righteous, blessed are all who walk in the ways of righteousness, in whom there are no sins like those of sinners, when all their days are numbered.

5 Concerning the progress of the sun in heaven, it goes in and out of each gate for thirty days, with the leaders of the thousand classes of the stars, with four days which are added, and divide the four quarters of the year which they conduct, and come with the four days.

6 Men greatly err concerning these, and count them not in the account of the course of the world, for they greatly err concerning them, and they are not exactly shewn to men, but they are in the account of the course of the world, and certainly they are united together for ever, one in the first gate, one in the third, one in the fourth, and one in the sixth.

7 And the year is finished in three hundred and sixty-four days.

8 And truly this is an exact and just account of their stations which is put together, for the lights, the months, the appointed times, the years, and the days Uriel has shewed, and communicated to me, whom for me the Lord of the creation of the world, according to the power of heaven, and the dominion which it possesses both by day and by night, commanded to explain to man the laws of the light of the sun, moon, and stars, and of all the powers of heaven, which are turned round in their orbits.

9 And these are the orders of the stars, which set in their places, in their times, in their appointed days, and in their months.

10 And these are the names of those who conduct them, who watch and come in their times, according to their order, in their periods, in their months, in their power, and in their places.

11 Four conductors of them come first, who divide the four quarters of the year, and after these twelve conductors of their orders, who divide the months and the year into three hundred and sixty-four days, with the leaders of a thousand, who divide the days, and the four which are joined among them, which as conductors divide the four quarters of the year.

12 These leaders of a thousand are in the midst of the conductors, and the conducting, and the conductors each at his place make the division. These are the names of the conductors who divide the four quarters of the year, who are appointed; Melkel, Helammelek,

13 Melial, and Narel.

14 And the names of those who conduct them are Adnarel, Jyasusael, and Jyelumiel.

15 These are the three which follow after the conductors of the orders, each following after the three conductors of the orders, which themselves follow after these conductors of the places, who divide the four quarters of the year.

16 In the first part of the year Melkias rises, and rules, who also is called Temani, and the sun.

17 All the days of his power, which he rules are ninety-one days.

18 And these are the signs which are seen on earth in the days of his power, perspiration, heat, and trouble, all the trees become fruitful, the leaf of every tree goes forth, the wheat is reaped, the rose and. every species of flowers blossom in the fields, and the trees of winter are dry.

19 And these are the names of the conductors who are under them: Barkel, Zelsabel, and another conductor of a thousand is added, whose name is Heloyaleph, and at the end of the days of his power, the conductor after him Helemmelek, by name they call the splendid sun.

20 And all the days of his light are ninety-nine days.

21 And these are the signs of the days upon the earth, heat, and drought, and the trees bring forth their fruits wanned, and concocted, and give their fruits to dry.

22 The flocks follow and receive, and all the fruits of the earth are gathered, and all which is in the fields, and the winepress is trodden, and this is done in the days of his power.

23 These are their names and orders, and the conductors who are under them, who are chiefs of thousands, are Gedaeyel, Keel, and Heel.

24 And a leader of a thousand is added to them whose name is Asphael.

25 And to the end of these are the days of his power.

CHAP. XXXIV.

1 And now my son Mathusala, I have shewn thee every sight which I saw before thee, I will relate two visions which I saw before I took a wife, and one of them is not like the other.

2 The first was when I learned a book, the other before I took thy mother. I saw a powerful vision,

3 And by reason of that besought the Lord.

4 When I rested in the house of my grandfather Malaleel, I saw in a vision heaven purified, and taken away.

5 I fell on the earth, and when I fell, I saw the earth swallowed up in a great abyss, and mountains suspended over mountains.

6 Hills were sinking upon hills, lofty trees were cut off from their roots, and were thrown, and sunk in the abyss.

7 Therefore the word fell down in my mouth, I raised a cry, and said, The earth is destroyed. And when I baa called my grandfather Malaleel, he raised me up, and said to me, Wherefore criest thou so, my son? and wherefore lamentest thou in this manner?

8 And I related to him all the vision which I had seen. He said to me, It is ponderous what thou sayest, my son;

9 And the vision of thy dream is powerful concerning every secret sin of the earth, for it shall be plunged into the abyss, and sink below into a great destruction.

10 Now my son rise up, and beseech the Lord of glory, (for thou art faithful) that a remnant may remain on the earth, and that he will not destroy it all. My son all this evil upon the earth is caused by heaven, for there shall be a great destruction upon the earth.

11 Then I arose, prayed, and intreated, and wrote down my prayer for the generation of the world, and I have shewed all to thee Mathusala, my son.

12 And I went out below, and saw the heaven and the sun going forth from the east, and every star, and the whole earth, and all which he has known from the beginning. I praised the Lord of judgment, and magnified him, because he has sent forth the sun from the windows of the east, that ascending and rising in the face of heaven, it might spring up, and go the way which for it had been appointed.

13 I lifted up my hands in righteousness, and praised the holy and the great One. I spake with the breath of my mouth, and with a tongue of flesh, which God has made for all the children of flesh, the men, that with it they may speak, and he gave them breath, a mouth, and a tongue, that with them they might speak.

14 Praised be you, O Lord the King, great and powerful in your greatness, Lord of all the creatures of heaven, King of Kings, whose kingdom, whose dominion, and whose majesty, remain through all eternity.

15 Your dominion is from generation to generation, and all the heavens are your throne for ever, and all the earth your footstool for ever and ever.

16 For you have made them, and over all you reign, and to you no work is difficult, for with you wisdom remains, and is always before your throne, and before your presence, you know all things, you see and hear them, and nothing can be concealed from you, for you understand all things.

17 And now the angels of your heavens have offended and on the flesh of men your wrath shall remain, until the day of the great judgment.

18 And now O God, Lord, and mighty King, I supplicate and pray you to grant me my petition, that you will leave to me a remnant of posterity upon the earth, and that you will not destroy all the flesh of men.

19 And that you will not leave the earth destitute, and that destruction may not be for ever,

20 And now my Lord, destroy from the earth the flesh which has offended you, but from the flesh of righteousness and integrity, establish you a plant of seed for ever. Lord, hide not your face from the prayer of your servant.

CHAP. XXXV.

1 After this, I saw another dream, and I explained it all to thee my son. Enoch arose and said to his son Mathusala, To thee my son I will speak. Hear my word, and incline thine ear to the vision of the dream of thy father. Before I took thy mother Edna, I saw a vision on my bed.

2 And behold, an animal went forth from the earth;

3 And this animal was white;

4 Afterward a female heifer went forth, and with it went forth a pair of animals, one of them was black, and the other red.

5 And that black animal struck the red one, and followed it over the earth.

6 From that time, I never could see the red animal, but the black one increased, and a female heifer came with him.

7 After this I saw that from him came forth many animals like him, and following after him.

8 The first female young one went out from the presence of the first animal, and sought the red animal, but found him not.

9 And she lamented with a great lamentation, and sought him.

10 And I saw that the first animal came to her afterwards, and made her quiet, and from that time she cried no more.

11 Afterwards she brought forth another white animal,

12 And after him brought forth many animals, and black cows.

13 And I saw in my sleep a white bull, which in like manner grew and became a great white bull.

14 After him came forth many animals like him.

15 And they began to shew many white animals which were like them, and followed each other.

16 Again I saw with my eyes while I slept, and I saw heaven above.

17 And behold a star fell from heaven,

18 And it raised itself up, and eat, and fed amongst these animals.

19 After that I saw other large and black animals, and behold they all changed their stalls, and pastures, and their young began to lament one with another. Again I saw in my vision, and looked to heaven, and behold, I saw many stars, which descended, and cast themselves from heaven to that first star,

20 Among these young cows, and the animals were with them and fed in the midst of them.

21 I looked at them and saw them, and behold they brought out their shame like those of horses, and began to ascend the young cows of the animals, and they all became pregnant, and brought elephants, camels and asses.

22 All the animals were afraid, and terrified for these, and they began to bite with their teeth, and to swallow them up, and to push with their horns.

23 They also began to devour the animals, and behold all the children of the earth began to tremble, and to quake for them, and to flee away.

24 Again I saw them when they began to push one another, and to swallow each other, and the earth began to cry out. And I raised my eyes again to heaven and saw in the vision, and behold, there came forth from heaven, as it were the appearance of white men. One came from that place, and three with him.

25 And those three who came forth last, took me by my hand, and raised me up from the generations of the earth, and exalted me to a high place.

26 And they shewed me a lofty tower on the earth, and every hill appeared to be less, and they said to me, remain here, until thou seest what will come upon these elephants, camels, and asses, upon the stars, and upon all the animals.

27 And I saw one of these four, who were come forth before.

28 He seized the first star, which fell down from heaven,

29 And he bound him hand and foot, and cast him into a cavern, a cavern narrow, and deep, dismal, and gloomy.

30 And one of them drew his sword, and gave it to these elephants, camels, and asses, and they began to smite one another, and beneath them the whole earth was shaken.

31 And then I saw in the vision, and behold the leader of these four angels, who were come, and descended from heaven, gathered together, and took all those great stars, whose shame were as the shame of horses, and bound them hand and foot, and cast them into the cavities of the earth.

CHAP. XXXVI.

1 And one of these four went to the white animals, and taught them a mystery, during which time the animal trembled, and it was born, and began to be a man, and built for himself a large ark, and in this he remained, and three animals remained with them in that ark, and there was a cover over them.

2 Again I lifted up my eyes to heaven, and saw a high roof and seven cataracts above it, which poured forth on a certain village much water.

3 And I looked again, and behold there were fountains open in the earth in that great village.

4 And the water began to boil up, and to rise over the earth, and that village could not be seen, for all its ground was covered with water.

5 And there was much water over it, and darkness and clouds, and I saw the height of this water, and it was above the height of the village.

6 And it overflowed the height of the village, and stood above all the earth.

7 And I saw that all the animals which had been gathered together in that village, were drowned, swallowed up, and destroyed in that water.

8 But the ark swam above the water; and all the animals, the elephants, the camels, and the asses were drowned upon the earth, and all cattle, and I could not see them again, for they were not able to get out, but went below, and sunk into the deep.

9 And again I saw in the vision that the cataracts were removed from that high roof, the fountains of the earth were turned back, and other depths were opened.

10 And the water began to descend into these until the dry land appeared.

11 The ark remained on the earth, the darkness was turned back, and it became light.

12 Then the white animal which became a man went out of the ark, and the three animals with him.

13 And one of the three animals was white like that animal, and one of them was red as blood, and one of them was black, and the white animal went away from them.

14 And wild beasts of the field, and birds began to bring forth.

15 The different kinds of these gathered together, lions, tigers, dogs, wolves, wild boars, foxes, rabbits, and swine.

16 And the siset, vultures, gledes, the phonkas, and ravens.

17 And a white animal was born in the midst of them.

18 And they began to bite one another, and the white animal which was born in the midst of them, produced a wild ass, and a white animal with him, and after that many wild asses, and the white animal which was born, brought forth a black wild boar, and a white sheep.

19 That wild boar brought forth many swine,

20 And that sheep brought forth twelve sheep.

21 When these twelve sheep were grown up, they delivered one of them to the asses.

22 Again the asses delivered that sheep to the wolves.

23 And he increased in the midst of the wolves.

24 And the Lord brought the eleven sheep, that they might dwell with him, and feed in the middle of the wolves.

25 And they multiplied, and there was plenty of pasture for them.

26 But the wolves began to frighten and oppress them, while they destroyed their young.

27 And they cast their young into streams of deep water.

28 And the sheep began to cry out on account of their young, and fled to their Lord, and a sheep which went with the wolves, escaped, and went away to the wild asses.

29 And I saw the sheep lament, and cry, and petition their Lord,

30 With all their power, till at their call the Lord of the sheep descended from his elevated mansion, and went to them, and beheld them.

31 And he called that sheep, who had secretly forsaken the wolves, and told him to declare to the wolves, that they were not to touch the sheep.

32 And that sheep went to the wolves with the word of the Lord, and another sheep met him, and went with him.

33 They both together came to the dwelling of the wolves, and spake with them, and declared to them, that from thence forward they should not touch the sheep.

34 And afterward I saw that the wolves with all their power were very severe against the sheep, but they cried, and their Lord came to the sheep.

35 He began to strike the wolves, who began to lament, but the sheep were quiet, and from that time they cried no more.

36 And I saw the sheep until they went out from the wolves, but the eyes of the wolves were blind for they went forth and followed the sheep with all their power, but the Lord of the sheep went with them, and conducted them.

37 And all his sheep followed him.

38 And his countenance was splendid and terrific, and his aspect was glorious, yet the wolves began to follow the sheep until they came near them in a sea of water.

CHAP. XXXVII.

1 Then that sea of water went back, the water stood hither and thither before their face,

2 And while their Lord conducted them, he placed himself between them and the wolves.

3 The wolves however saw not the sheep, but went into the midst of the sea of water, and they followed the sheep and ran after them in the sea of water.

4 But when they saw the Lord of the sheep, they turned themselves to fly from before his face.

5 Then the water of the sea turned again quickly, according to its nature, for it went forth, and rose up, until it covered the wolves, and I saw that all the wolves perished, and were drowned, that followed the sheep.

6 But the sheep went away from this water, and tarried in a desert in which there was neither water or grass, and they began to open their eyes, and to see.

7 And I saw that the Lord of the sheep looked after them, and gave them water and grass.

8 And that sheep continually went and led them.

9 And when he had ascended up to the top of a lofty rock, the Lord of the sheep sent him to them.

10 And after that I saw the Lord of the sheep stand before them and his countenance was terrible and strong.

11 And when all the sheep saw him, they were afraid at his appearance,

12 They were all afraid and trembled before him, and they cried out to that sheep who had been with him, and to the other who was in the midst of them, saying, We are not able to stand before our Lord, or to look upon him.

13 Then that sheep who conducted them turned back, and ascended the top of that rock.

14 But the sheep began to blind their eyes, and to turn from the path which he had shewn them, but he knew it not.

15 The Lord of the sheep was moved with great indignation against them, and when that sheep had learned what was done,

16 He descended from the top of the rock, and came to them, and found that there were a great number of them

17 Who had blinded their eyes,

18 And had turned from his path, and when they saw him they feared, and trembled at his presence,

19 And desired to turn back to their fold.

20 Then that sheep took with him other sheep, and came to those who had turned back,

21 And afterwards began to kill them, and they were afraid at his countenance, then he caused those who had gone away to return back, who went to their fold.

22 And I also saw in my vision, that this sheep became a man, built a house for the Lord of the sheep, and all the sheep stood in that house.

23 And I saw that the sheep died who went forth to meet the conductor of the sheep, and I saw that all the great sheep perished, and lesser ones rose up in their places, and came into a pasture, and drew near to a river of water.

24 Then that sheep who had conducted them, who became a man, was separated from them and died.

25 All the sheep sought him, and cried over him with a great cry.

26 I also saw that they left off crying after that sheep, and went over the river of water.

27 And there arose other sheep, all of whom conducted them, of the plant of those who were dead, and had conducted them.

28 Then I saw that the sheep came to a good place, and to a delightful and glorious land.

29 I also saw that the sheep became satiated, that their house was in the middle of a delightful land, that at times their eyes were opened, and at times they were blind, until another sheep arose, and conducted them. He brought them all back, and their eyes were opened.

30 Then dogs, foxes, and wild swine began to devour them, until another sheep arose, the lord of the flock, one of themselves, a ram to conduct them, and this ram began to toss hither and thither those dogs, foxes, and wild swine, until they all perished.

31 But the former sheep opened his eyes, and saw the ram in the midst of the sheep who had laid aside his glory.

32 And he began to push the sheep, and to tread on them, and to go on without honour.

33 Then the Lord of the sheep sent the former sheep again to another, and raised him up to be a ram, to conduct the sheep instead of that sheep who had laid aside his glory;

34 Therefore he went to him, and talked to him alone, and raised up that ram, and made him a prince and a leader of the flock, all the time that the dogs troubled the sheep.

35 And the first ram persecuted the latter ram.

36 Then the latter ram arose, and fled from before his face, and I saw that these dogs caused the first ram to fall.

37 But the latter ram arose, and conducted the smaller sheep.

38 That ram also begat many sheep and died.

CHAP. XXXVIII.

1 Then there was a smaller sheep, a ram, in his place, who became a prince, and a conductor of the sheep.

2 And these sheep increased, and multiplied.

3 And all the dogs, foxes, and wild swine feared, and fled from him.

4 And that ram also struck and killed all the wild beasts, so that they could not again come into the middle of the sheep, nor at any time take them away.

5 And that house was made great and wide, and a high tower was built upon that house by the sheep, for the Lord of the sheep.

6 The house was low, but the tower was elevated, and very high.

7 And the Lord of the sheep stood upon that tower, and they brought a full table before him.

8 Again I saw that those sheep turned, and went many ways, and forsook that house of the Lord.

9 And their Lord called to some in the midst of them, and sent them to the sheep.

10 But the sheep began to kill them, and when one of them was saved, and was not killed, he arose, and cried out against the sheep, who desired to kill him,

11 But the Lord of the sheep delivered him out of their hands, and caused him to ascend to him, still there to remain.

12 And he also sent many others to the sheep, to bear witness and to lament over them.

13 And I also saw that they forsook the house of the Lord of the sheep, by reason of their turnings, and blinding their eyes.

14 And I saw that the Lord of the sheep made a great slaughter among them in their pasture, until the sheep cried out to him by reason of that slaughter, and he gave up the praise of that place, and left them in the power of lions, tigers, wolves, and in the power of foxes, and of every beast of the field.

15 And the wild beasts of the field began to tear the sheep.

16 And I also saw that he forsook the house of their fathers, and their tower, and gave them all into the power of lions, to tear and to devour them, and into the power of every beast.

17 Then I began to cry with all my power, and cried to the Lord of the sheep, and shewed that the sheep were devoured by all the beasts of the field.

18 But in silence he beheld it, and rejoiced because they were devoured, swallowed up, and carried away, and he left them in the power of the beasts for food. He called also seventy shepherds, and gave up to them the sheep, that they might overlook them.

19 And he said to the shepherds, and to their servants, From henceforth every one of you overlook the sheep, and do all that I command you, and I will deliver them to you by number.

20 And I will tell you which of them shall go down, these destroy, and he delivered to them the sheep.

21 Then he called to another, and said, Understand and see everything which the shepherds shall do to these sheep, for among them there shall many more perish than I have commanded,

22 And every excess and slaughter which the shepherds shall commit shall be written down, as, how many they have destroyed at my command, and how many they have destroyed of their own heads.

23 And there shall be a written account of all the destruction by each of the shepherds, according to the number read before me, how many they have destroyed of their own heads, and how many they have delivered up to destruction, that I may have this testimony against them, that I may know all the deeds of the shepherds, and that delivering the sheep to them, I may see whether they will do according to my command, which I commanded them or not.

24 They shall not understand this, and thou shalt not make them to understand, neither shalt thou reprove them. But all the destruction of the shepherds every one in his time shall be written down, and brought to me. And I saw that there was an inspection of the shepherds at that time. Then they began to kill, and to destroy more than was commanded.

25 And they left the sheep in the power of the lions, and the greatest part of them were devoured and swallowed up by lions and tigers, and wild boars destroyed them. They burnt that tower, and overthrew that house.

26 And I was very sorrowful on account of the tower, and because the house of the sheep was overthrown.

27 And afterwards I was not able to see that house.

28 And the shepherds and their servants gave these sheep to all the wild beasts, that they might devour them, and every one of them in his time and number was given up, and each of them one with another was described in a book, and how many of them one with another were destroyed, was described in a book.

29 But every shepherd killed, and destroyed more than was commanded.

30 Then I began to weep, and was very angry on account of the sheep.

31 And I also saw in the vision him who wrote, how he wrote down one destroyed by the shepherds every day, and he ascended, remained, and shewed all his book to the Lord of the

sheep, containing all which they had done, and all which each of them had put away from them,

32 And all which they had given up to destruction.

33 And the book was read before the Lord of the sheep, for he took up the book in his hands, and read it, and sealed it, and placed it there.

34 After this I saw the conducting shepherds inspecting for twelve hours.

35 And behold three of the sheep turned, and came, and went in, and began to build all that was fallen down of that house.

36 But the boars of the field hindered them, but they prevailed not.

37 Again they began to build as before, and raised up that tower, which was called a high tower.

38 And again they began to place before the tower a table, with every kind of bread thereon, which was impure and unclean.

39 Moreover the eyes of the sheep were blind, and they could not see, and the shepherds also were blind.

40 And they were delivered up to the shepherds for the destruction of a great number, who trod the sheep under foot, and devoured them.

41 Yet the Lord was silent until all the sheep of the fields were diminished. The shepherds and the sheep were mixed together, but they delivered them not from the power of the beasts.

42 Then he who wrote the book ascended, and shewed, and read it at the mansion of the Lord of the sheep, and on their account he petitioned him, and prayed, and shewed all the deeds of the shepherds, and testified before him against them all. Then he took the book, and deposited it near him, and departed.

CHAP. XXXIX.

1 And I saw that up to the time in such a manner, thirty-seven conducting shepherds inspected, and they all finished in their times as the first, and others then received them into their

hands, that they might inspect them in their times, every shepherd in his time.

2 And after that, I saw in the vision, that all the birds of heaven came, eagles, vultures, kites, and ravens, and the eagle taught them all.

3 They began to devour the sheep, to pick out their eyes, and to devour their bodies.

4 And the sheep cried out, because their bodies were devoured by the birds.

5 I also cried out, and groaned in my sleep against that shepherd which inspected the flock,

6 And I looked till the sheep were eaten up by the dogs, by the eagles, and by the kites, and they left them neither body, nor skin, nor muscles, until their bones alone stood there, and their bones fell upon the earth, and the sheep were diminished.

7 And I saw during one time that twenty-three conducting shepherds inspected, who completed in their times fifty-eight times.

8 Then small lambs were born of those white sheep, and they began to open their eyes, and to see, and to cry out to the sheep.

9 But the sheep cried not out to them, and they heard not what they said, but were extremely deaf, and powerfully and strongly blinded their eyes.

10 I saw in the vision that ravens flew down upon these lambs,

11 And that they took one of these lambs, and they tare the sheep in pieces and devoured them.

12 And I saw that horns grew forth upon these lambs, and that the searching ravens came down upon these horns,

13 And I saw that a large horn sprouted forth on one of the sheep, and their eyes were opened,

14 And he looked at them, and placed himself before their eyes, and he cried to the sheep.

15 Then the dabela saw him, and they all ran to him.

16 And contempt of these brought all the eagles, vultures, ravens, and kites, around the sheep, and they flew down upon

them, and devoured them, and the sheep were silent, but the dabela lamented and cried out.

17 Then the ravens fought and struggled with them.

18 They wished among them to remove that horn, but they overcame him not.

19 I looked at them until the shepherds, the eagles, the vultures, and the kites came,

20 And they cried out to the ravens to break the horn of the dabela, to contend with him, and to fight with him, but he struggled with them, and cried out that his help might come to him.

21 Then I looked until the man came who had written down the names of the shepherds, and who ascended up before the Lord of the sheep.

22 He brought assistance and caused every one to see him descend to the help of the dabela.

23 And I saw that the Lord of the sheep came to them in his wrath, and all those who saw him fled away, and all fell down in his tabernacle before his face, and all the eagles, vultures, ravens, and kites assembled together, and brought with them all the sheep of the field.

24 And they all came assembled together, and strove to break the horn of the dabela.

25 And I also saw that to them came the Lord of the sheep, and took in his hand the sceptre of his wrath, and smote the earth, which was rent asunder, and all the beasts and birds of heaven fell down from the sheep, and sunk into the earth, and there they were buried.

26 And I also saw that a mighty sword was given to the sheep, who went forth against all the beasts of the field to destroy them.

27 But all the beasts and birds of heaven fled from before their face.

28 Then I saw that the man who wrote the book at the word of the Lord, opened the book of destruction, of those who had been destroyed by the last twelve shepherds, and shewed before the Lord of the sheep, that they had destroyed more than those who had been before them.

29 I stood and saw till he took down that ancient house, and they brought out its pillars, every plant, and the ivory of that house, with which it was overlaid, they brought it out and laid it on a place on the right side of the earth.

30 And I beheld the Lord of the sheep, until he produced anew house, greater and higher than the first, and he set it upon the place of the first, which was covered, and all its pillars were new, and its ivory new, and stronger than the first ivory, which he had brought out.

31 And the Lord of the sheep was in the middle, and I saw all the sheep which remained, and all the beasts of the earth, and fowls of heaven, fell down, and cast themselves before the sheep, and supplicated them, and heard them in every word.

32 And the sheep were all white, with their wool long and clean, and all who had perished, and had been destroyed, and all the beasts of the field, and all the fowls of heaven, turned back to that house, and the Lord of the sheep rejoiced with great joy, because they were all good, and had turned back again to his dwelling.

33 And I saw that they laid down the sword which had been given to the sheep, and brought it back to his house, and sealed it up in the presence of the Lord.

34 All the sheep were enclosed in that house, but it did not contain them all at one time, and the eyes of all were open, and they saw the good One, and there was none among them who did not behold him.

35 And I saw that this house was great and wide and very full, and I saw that a white being was born, whose horns were great, and that all the beasts of the field and the fowls of heaven feared him, and prayed to him at all times.

36 Then I saw that the nature of them all was changed, and that they all became white animals.

37 And that the first who was in the midst of them became a Word, and that Word became a large being, and on his head were great horns.

38 And the Lord of the sheep rejoiced over them, and over all the animals.

39 I reposed in the middle of them, I awoke and saw the whole, and this is the vision which I saw while I slept, and when I awaked, I praised the Lord of righteousness, and gave him glory.

40 Then those three who were clothed in white, who before had caused me to ascend, they held me by my hand, and the hand of him who spake held me, and they raised me up, and set me in the middle of the sheep before the judgment began.

41 And I saw a throne erected in a delightful land;

42 Upon this sat the Lord of the sheep, and received all the sealed books.

43 And these books were opened before the Lord of the sheep.

44 Then the Lord called the first seven white ones, and commanded them to bring before him the first of the stars, which went before the stars whose shame were like the shame of horses, and the first star which fell down first, and they brought them all before him.

45 And he spake to that man who wrote before him who was one of the seven white ones, and said, Take those seventy shepherds, to whom I delivered the sheep, and who received them, and killed more than those which I had commanded them, and be. hold, I saw them all bound, and all stand before him. And the judgment of the stars came on first, and they were all judged, and found guilty, and went to the place of punishment, and they thrust them into a deep full of burning fire, and full of pillars of fire. Then the seventy shepherds were judged, and were found guilty, and were thrust into the flaming abyss.

46 And I saw at that time, that in the middle of the earth one deep was opened which was full of fire,

47 And to this they brought the blind sheep, and they were judged, and found guilty, and were all thrust into the deep of fire on the earth, and burnt.

48 And this deep was on the right side of that house.

49 And I saw the sheep burning, and their bones consuming.

50 Afterwards I wept a great weeping, and my tears ceased not, so that I was not able to bear it, and when I looked, they

descended by reason of that which I had seen, for all was come and gone, for every particular part of the affairs of men was shewn to me.

51 In that night I remembered my former dream, therefore I wept and was troubled, because I had seen that vision.

CHAP. XL.

1 And now my son Mathusala, call to me all thy brethren, and gather to me all the children of thy mother, for a voice calls me, and the spirit is poured out upon me, that I may shew you every thing which shall happen to you for ever.

2 Then Mathusala went and called to him all his brethren, and gathered together all his relations.

3 And he spake to all his children in truth;

4 Enoch said, Hear my children every word of your father, and listen in uprightness to the voice of my mouth, for I would gain your attention, while to you I speak. My beloved, love integrity, and walk in it.

5 Approach not integrity with a double heart, and join not yourselves with those who are double hearted; but my children walk in righteousness, which will conduct you in good paths, and let truth be your companion.

6 For I know that the state of oppression will be powerful on earth, and that it will be terminated by a great punishment on the earth, and there shall be an end of all unrighteousness which shall be cut off from its root, and all its fabric shall pass away. But unrighteousness shall be renewed again, and stand forth upon the earth, for every work of unrighteousness, and every work of oppression, and crime, shall be taken hold of a second time.

7 Therefore when unrighteousness, sin, blasphemy, oppression, and every evil work shall increase, and also when transgression, impiety, and uncleanness shall increase, then upon them all there shall be inflicted a great punishment from heaven.

8 The holy Lord will go forth with wrath, and with punishment, that he may execute judgment on the earth.

9 In those days oppression shall be cut off from its roots, and the roots of iniquity together with fraud shall be rooted out from under heaven.

10 Every place of strength with its multitude shall be given up, and shall be burnt with fire.

11 And they shall be brought from all the earth, and be cast into a judgment of fire, and they shall perish in wrath, and by a powerful judgment for ever.

12 And the righteous shall be raised up from slumbers and wisdom shall be raised up, and shall be given to them.

13 Then the roots of wickedness shall be cut off, and sinners shall perish by the sword, and blasphemers in every part shall be destroyed.

14 Those who meditate oppression, and those who blaspheme shall perish by the sword.

15 And now my children, I will describe and shew to you the way of righteousness, and the way of oppression.

16 I will again point them out to you, that ye may know what is to come.

17 And now hear my children and walk in the way of righteousness, but go not in the way of oppression, for all who walk in the ways of iniquity shall; perish for ever.

CHAP. XLI.

1 That was written by Enoch. He wrote all his instruction of wisdom for every man of renown, and for every judge of the earth, for all his children who shall dwell on the earth, and for succeeding generations who shall work righteousness and peace.

2 Let not your spirit be sorrowful by reason of the times, for the holy, the great One has given days to all.

3 Let the righteous man arise from slumber, let him arise and walk in the ways of righteousness, and let his ways and his goings be in goodness and eternal clemency, for there shall be mercy for the righteous man, integrity and power shall be given to him for ever, he shall exist in goodness and in righteousness, and shall walk in everlasting light, but sin shall perish in eternal

darkness, and from this time forward shall be seen no more for ever.

4   After this, Enoch began to instruct from a book.

5   And Enoch said, Concerning the children of righteousness, concerning the elect of the world, and concerning the plant of righteousness and integrity;

6   Concerning these things I will speak, and declare to you my children, I who am Enoch. By reason of that which has appeared to me in my heavenly visions, and from the voice of the holy angels I have obtained knowledge, and from the tablet of heaven I have obtained understanding.

7   Enoch then began to instruct from a book, and said, I have been born the seventh in the first week, so long as judgment and righteousness were with patience.

8   But after me in the second week, great wickedness shall arise, and deceit shall shoot forth.

9   In that week will be the end of the first, in which mankind will be safe.

10 But when the second is completed, wickedness shall increase, and in the third week he shall execute the decree upon sinners.

11 Afterwards in the accomplishment of the third week a man for a plant of the judgment of righteousness shall be chosen, and after him the plant of righteousness shall come for ever.

12 Afterwards in the accomplishment of the fourth week, the visions of the holy and the righteous shall be seen, and the law from generation to generation, and a tabernacle shall be made for them; and after this in the accomplishment of the fifth week, the house of glory and dominion shall be erected for ever.

13 After that in the sixth week, all who are in it shall be darkened, and the hearts of them all will forget wisdom, and in it a man shall ascend to heaven.

14 And in its accomplishment the house of dominion shall be burnt with fire, and in the same the whole generation of the elect root shall be dispersed.

15 Afterwards, in the seventh week, a perverse generation shall arise, its deeds shall be many, and all its deeds perverse, but in its accomplishment the righteous chosen from the plants

of eternal righteousness shall be rewarded, and to them shall be given sevenfold instruction concerning all his creation.

16 And afterwards there shall be another week, the eighth of righteousness, in which a sword shall be given to execute judgment and justice on all oppressors.

17 And sinners shall be delivered into the hands of the righteous, and in its accomplishment they shall obtain habitations by their righteousness, and the house of the great King shall be built up for ever. And after that, in the ninth week, the judgment of righteousness shall be revealed to the whole world.

18 And all the works of the ungodly shall vanish away from all the earth, the destruction of the world shall be appointed, and all men shall look out for the way of righteousness.

19 And after this on the seventh day of the tenth week, there shall be an everlasting judgment, which shall be executed upon the watchers, and an extensive heaven shall spring forth in the middle of the angels, which shall remain for evermore.

20 The former heaven shall depart and pass away, a new heaven shall appear, and all the heavenly powers shall shine with sevenfold splendor for ever, and afterwards there shall be weeks without number, which shall exist in goodness and in righteousness for evermore.

21 And from that time sin shall not be mentioned there for ever and ever.

22 And who is there of all the children of men, who is able to hear the voice of the holy One, and not to be agitated?

23 And who is there that is able to think his thoughts? Who is able to behold all the work of the beautiful heavens? And who is there that can understand the deeds of heaven?

24 He may behold its animation, but not its spirit, and he may be able to speak about it, but he cannot ascend to it, and he may see the boundaries of these things, and consider them, but he can make nothing like them.

25 And who is there among all men who is able to understand the breadth and length of the earth?

26 And by whom hath the greatness of all these things been shewn? Is it every man who is able to know the extent of heaven, and find out its elevation, and whereon it is made to remain?

27 And how great is the number of the stars? And where is the rest of the lights of heaven?

CHAP. XLII.

1 And now my children, I desire you to love righteousness, and to walk in it, for the paths of righteousness are worthy of being received, but the paths of iniquity shall suddenly be undone, and be diminished.

2 The ways of oppression and death have been shewn to men distinguished in their generation, but they keep far from them, and follow them not.

3 And now I declare to you, to the righteous, Go not in the ways of wickedness and oppression, nor in the ways of death, come not nigh them, that you may not perish, but desire,

4 And choose for yourselves righteousness, and a pleasant life.

5 And go in the ways of peace, that ye may live, and be found worthy; retain my words in the thoughts of your hearts, and destroy them not from your hearts, for I know that sinners cause men to execute wicked deceit. They will not come to every place, nor is every consultation diminished by them.

6 Wo to them who build up wickedness, and oppression, and who lay the foundation of deceit, for they shall be suddenly overthrown, and to them there shall be no peace.

7 Wo to them who build up their houses with sin, for from their foundations they shall be overthrown, and they shall fall by the sword. And they who possess gold and silver gotten by injustice shall suddenly perish in judgment. Wo to you who are rich, for upon your riches you have confided, but from your riches you shall be removed, because you have not remembered the Most High in the days of your riches.

8 You have committed blasphemy, and wickedness, and are prepared for the day of the shedding of blood, to the day of darkness, and to the day of the great judgment.

9 This I declare and point out to you, that he who created you will destroy you.

10 And over your fall there will be no compassion, but your creator will rejoice at your destruction.

11 And in those days your righteous shall be a disgrace to sinners and to the ungodly.

12 O that my eyes were clouds of water, that I might weep over you, and let my tears flow like a cloud of water, and rest from the sorrow of my heart.

13 Who has permitted you to practise hatred and wickedness, the judgment shall extend to you, ye sinners.

14 The righteous shall not be afraid before sinners, because the Almighty again will bring them into your hands, that ye may take vengeance of them according to your pleasure.

15 Wo unto you who are so execrable by execrations, that you cannot be set free, and the remedy is far from you by reason of your sins. Wo unto you who reward your neighbour with evil, for you shall be rewarded according to your works.

16 Wo to you ye witnesses of falsehood, and those who declare unrighteousness, for you shall suddenly perish.

17 Wo to you ye sinners, for you expel the righteous, for you receive or expel at pleasure those who work wickedness, and their yoke shall be heavy upon you.

18 Wait in hope, ye righteous, for suddenly the sinners shall be destroyed before you, and you shall have dominion over them according to your will.

19 In the day of the affliction of sinners your offspring shall be exalted, and lifted up like eagles, and your nest shall be higher than that of the vultures, you shall ascend and enter into the holes of the earth, and into the clefts of the rocks for ever, like rabbits from the sight of the unrighteous.

20 And they shall groan over you, and weep like sirens.

21 And you shall not fear those who trouble you, for there shall be healing for you, a brilliant light shall shine around, and the voice of peace shall be heard from heaven. Wo to you ye sinners, for your riches make you like the righteous, but your hearts reproach you that you are sinners. This word shall be a witness against you for the remembrance of wickedness.

22 Wo to you who feed upon the best of the wheat, and drink the strength of the root of the spring, and in your power tread down the humble.

23 Wo to you who drink water at pleasure, for suddenly you shall be rewarded, for ye shall be consumed, and withered, because ye have forgotten the fountain of life.

24 Wo to you, who practice wickedness, deceit, and blasphemy, there shall be a remembrance against you for the evil.

25 Wo to you, ye mighty, who with your power strike down righteousness, for the day of your destruction shall come, but at that time, the time of your judgment, there shall be many and delightful days for the righteous.

CHAP. XLIII.

1 The righteous are confident that sinners will be put to shame, and perish in the day of wickedness.

2 To you that shall be known, for the Most High will remember your destruction, and over that destruction the angels will rejoice. What will ye do, ye sinners, and where will ye fly in the day of judgment, when you shall hear the words of the prayer of the righteous.

3 And ye shall not be like them, who shall be witness against you with these words, Ye were companions of sinners.

4 And in those days the prayers of the righteous shall come up before the Lord, and when the day of your judgment shall come, and every word of your wickedness shall be declared before the great and holy One,

5 Your faces shall be ashamed, when ye shall be rejected for every deed, which is strong in wickedness.

6 Wo to you, ye sinners, for in the middle of the sea, and on the dry land, there is an evil report against you. Wo to you, who have in your possession silver and gold not obtained in righteousness, and say, We are rich, have obtained wealth, and we have possession of all that we can desire:

7 And now we will do what we are inclined, for we have gathered silver, our barns are full, and the husbandmen of our household are like much water.

8 Your falsehood shall flow away like water, for your riches shall not remain, but shall suddenly ascend from you, because ye have obtained it all in unrighteousness; you shall be appointed to extreme malediction.

9 And now I declare to you ye cunning and foolish, because ye often view the earth, and because ye men, spread more ornaments over you than any young woman, every where arraying yourselves in majesty, in elevation, in magnificence, in authority, and in silver; but gold, purple, honour, and riches, like water shall flow away.

10 Therefore instruction and wisdom are not in them, and by this they shall perish, together with all their riches, with all their splendour, and with all their honours.

11 And in disgrace, and in slaughter, and in extreme poverty, your spirits shall be cast into a furnace of fire.

12 I have declared to you ye sinners, that neither mountain or hill has been or shall be a servant to women.

13 In one year such a mass of sin has not been sent upon the earth, but men of their own heads have caused it, and a powerful malediction shall be the portion of those who this have done.

14 And barrenness shall not be inflicted upon women, but on account of the works of their hands they shall die childless.

15 I have declared to you ye sinners, by the holy and great One, that all your evil deeds are revealed in the heavens, and that there is not one of the deeds of your oppression concealed and secret.

16 Think not in your spirits, neither say in your hearts, that every crime is not seen, and written down, for what is done is written every day before the Most High in heaven, and from this time forth it shall be marked down, for all your oppression with which you have oppressed, shall be written every day until the day of your judgment.

17 Wo to you, ye fools, for ye shall perish in your folly, for you will not listen to the wise, and what is good you shall not find out.

18 Now therefore know that you are appointed to the day of destruction, and expect not that sinners shall live, but you shall go on and die, for you are not pointed out for redemption.

19 But you are appointed for the day of the great judgment, for the day of tribulation, and the extreme disgrace of your souls.

20 Wo to you, ye hardened in heart, who commit wickedness and feed on blood. Whence do you eat and drink what is good, and are satiated? Is it not because our Lord the Most High has richly given every good thing on earth? To you there shall be no peace.

21 Wo to you who love the deeds of unrighteousness. Wherefore do ye expect that which is good? Know that you shall be given into the hands of the righteous who shall cut off your necks, kill you, and shew you no compassion.

22 Wo to you who have your joy at the trouble of the righteous, for a grave shall not be dug for you.

23 Wo to you who frustrate the word of the righteous, for to you there shall be no hope of life.

24 Wo to you who write down the word of falsehood, and the word of the ungodly, for they write down their falsehood, that they may hear, and not forget folly.

25 And for them there shall be no peace, for by death they shall suddenly expire.

CHAP. XLIV.

1 Wo to them who commit wickedness, who praise and honour the word of falsehood; you have been lost in your way, and there is not in you a good life.

2 Wo to you who change the words of righteousness, ye transgress the everlasting decree,

3 And make the heads of those who are not sinners to be trodden down upon the earth.

4 0 ye righteous, in those days ye shall have been thought worthy of having your prayers to rise up for a remembrance, and they shall be set for a witness before the angels, that they

may place the sins of sinners for a remembrance before the Most High.

5 In those days the nations shall be amazed, but the generations of the nations shall be raised again in the day of destruction.

6 And in those days they who shall become pregnant, shall go forth and tear their children, and forsake them, and their offspring shall fall from them, and while suckling them, they shall cast them away, and shall never return to them, and have no compassion for their beloved.

7 Again I declare to you ye sinners, that crime has been appointed for the day of blood, which never ceases.

8 They shall worship stones, and form images of gold, of silver, of wood, and of clay, and they shall worship unclean spirits, daemons, and every idol in temples, but no relief shall be found for them, and they shall become forgetful by reason of the folly of their hearts, and their eyes shall be blinded in the fears of their hearts, and in the visions of their dreams, in which they shall be wicked, and be afraid, because all their deeds are done in falsehood, and worshiping stones, and they shall be altogether destroyed.

9 But in those days they shall be blessed, who receive the word of wisdom, who proclaim and receive the way of the Most High, who walk in the ways of righteousness, and who are not wicked with those who are wicked.

10 Then they shall be secure.

11 Wo to you who extend the wickedness of your neighbour, for in hell you shall be destroyed.

12 Wo to you who lay the foundation of sin, and who are bitter upon earth, for upon it you shall be destroyed.

13 Wo to you who build your houses by the labour of others, and all its fabric is brick, and the stone of sin; to you I declare that peace you shall never obtain.

14 Wo to you, who consume the measure of the portion of your father, which is for ever, and your spirits follow after idols; for you there shall be no repose.

15 Wo to them who work wickedness, and give aid to oppression, who slay their neighbour until the day of the great

judgment, for your glory shall be cast down, malice shall be put in your hearts, and he shall stir up the spirit of his indignation, that he may destroy you all with the sword.

16 Then all the righteous and the holy shall remember your crimes.

17 And in those days fathers shall be slain with their children in one place, and brethren with their neighbours shall fall down in death, until a stream shall flow from their blood.

18 For a man shall not keep back his hand from his children, nor from his children's children, for he has been merciful, that he may kill them.

19 And the sinner shall not keep back his hand from his honoured brother, for the slaughter shall continue from the appearance of day to the setting of the sun, and the horse shall wade up to his breast, and the chariot shall sink to its upper part in the blood of sinners.

CHAP. XLV.

1 And in those days the angels shall descend into lurking holes, and bring together into one place all those who have assisted in sin.

2 In that day the Most High shall rise up to execute the great judgment upon all sinners, and he will appoint the holy angels to be watchers over all the righteous and the holy, that they may protect them as the pupil of an eye, until all wickedness and all sin be destroyed.

3 And then all the righteous shall sleep a deep sleep, for there is nothing in them to make them afraid, and truly they shall see the wise men.

4 And the children of the earth shall understand every word of that book, and know that their riches cannot save them from the ruin of their sins.

5 Wo to you, ye sinners, when ye shall be grieved before the righteous in the day of the violent oppression, ye shall be burnt in the fire, and rewarded according to your works.

6 Wo to you, ye corrupted in heart, who watch to understand wickedness, and to find out terrors, for you there will be no assistance.

7 Wo to you ye sinners, for on account of the words of your mouths, and the works of your hands, you have committed impiety, you shall be burnt in the heat of a flaming fire.

8 And now know ye, that the angels shall search out your deeds in heaven from the sun, and from the moon, and from the stars, on account of your wickedness; for upon the earth you exercised authority over the righteous.

9 Every cloud shall bear witness against you, the mist, and the dew, and the rain, they shall all be withholden from you, that they may not descend to you, and assist you because of your sins.

10 And now bring gifts to the Almighty for the rain, that it may not be withholden, but descend upon you, and for the dew, if you have received by it gold, or silver, but when the frost, snow, cold, and every snowy wind, and all their afflictions shall fall upon you, at that time, you shall not be able to stand before them.

11 Now seriously consider heaven, all ye children of heaven, and all ye works of the Most High, fear him, and do no evil before him.

12 When he shuts up the windows of heaven, and restrains the rain and the dew, that it may not descend on the earth on your account, what will ye do then?

13 And when he sends his indignation upon you, and upon all your works, you are not they who can intreat him, you who speak great and powerful things against his righteousness, and to you there shall be no peace.

14 And do you not behold the governors of ships, how their ships are driven about by the waves, torn to pieces by the winds, and exposed to danger?

15 Therefore they are afraid, because all their valuable riches are with them on the ocean, and they think not good in their hearts, because the sea may swallow them up, and in it they may be destroyed.

16 Is not the whole sea, all its waters, and all its commotions, the work of him the Most High? And he has sealed up all its operations, and enclosed it around with sand.

17 And at his rebuke it is dried up, and alarmed, and all which is in the same, and will ye not fear him ye sinners, who are upon the earth? Is he not the Creator of heaven and earth, and of all things which are in them?

18 And who has given instruction and wisdom to all those who are upon the earth, and to those on the sea?

19 Are not the governors of ships afraid of the ocean? And shall not sinners be afraid before the Most High?

CHAP. XLVI.

1 In those days when he shall bring upon you ardent fire, where will you fly, and where will you be secure?

2 And when he sends forth his word against you, are you not astonished and afraid?

3 All the luminaries are moved with great fear, and the whole earth is astonished, while it trembles, and suffers anxiety.

4 All the angels perform the commands which they have received, and desire to be concealed from the presence of the great glory, while the children of the earth tremble, and are agitated.

5 But you ye sinners are execrable for ever, for you there shall be no peace.

6 Fear not ye souls of the righteous, but hope for the day of your death in righteousness, and be not sorrowful, because in great trouble, with groaning, lamentation, and sorrow, your souls descend to the repository of the dead, for in your lives your bodies have not received according to your goodness, but in the days in which you existed, many more sinners existed, in the days of execration and punishment.

7 And when you die, the sinners say concerning you, As we die the righteous die: what advantage have they in their works? Behold like us they die in sorrow, and in darkness. What is their superiority before us? Henceforward we are equal, and from hence what will they obtain and what will they see for

ever? For behold they are dead, and from this time they never will again perceive the light. I say unto you ye sinners, Ye have been satisfied with meat, and drink, with spoil of men, with robbery, and sin, with the acquisition of wealth, and the sight of good days, but have you not seen the righteous, their end is in peace, because no oppression is found in them, even to the day of their death. They perish, and are as if they were not, while their souls descend in trouble to the repository of the dead.

8 But now I declare to you ye righteous, by his great splendour and glory, by his renowned kingdom, and by his majesty, to you I declare that I understand this mystery, that I have read on the tablets of heaven, and have seen the book of the holy Ones, and I have seen what is written and impressed upon them.

9 For all goodness, joy, and glory has been prepared for them, and written down for the spirits of them who die in righteousness, and much goodness. It shall be given to you a plant of your suffering, and your portion shall far exceed the portion of the living.

10 The spirits of you who die in righteousness shall live, and their spirits shall rejoice and exult, and their remembrance shall be before the face of the mighty One for all the generations of the world, and they shall not now fear their disgrace.

11 Wo to you ye sinners, when you die in your sins, and they who are like you say concerning you, Blessed are those sinners, they have seen all their days, and now they die in happiness, and in wealth, in their lives they saw not calamity and destruction, they die in honour, and in their lives they never were restrained by judgment.

12 But has it not been shewn to them, that when their souls shall be made to descend to the repository of the deed, their wickedness will then become their greatest torment, for their spirits shall enter into darkness, into the snare, end into the flame, which shall burn to the great judgment, and the great judgment shall be for all generations and for ever.

13 Wo to you, for to you there shall be no peace, and ye cannot say to the righteous, and to the good who are alive, In the

days of our distress we have been loaden with affliction, and every trouble we have seen, and much evil we have suffered;

14 And our spirits have been wasted, weakened, and diminished;

15 We have been sentenced to the lowest places, and there was nothing to help us in word or deed that we knew, and because we found none we have been oppressed, and condemned to misery.

16 We have not expected to live from day to day:

17 And we hoped to become the head,

18 But we have become the tail. We have been oppressed when we laboured, but we had no power over our oppressors, we have been food for sinners, and the yoke of the ungodly has been heavy upon us.

19 Those who hate and afflict us were powerful over us, and to those who hate us we had bowed our neck, but towards us there was no compassion.

20 We sought to go from them, that we might fly away, and have rest, but we found no place to which we could fly, and be secure from them. We have accursed them before princes in our distress, and have cried out to those who were devouring us, but they regarded not our cry, and they were not disposed to hear our voice.

21 But they assist those who rob and devour us, those who diminish us, and conceal their oppression, who remove not from us their yoke, but devour, enervate, and slay us, who conceal our slaughter, yet by that never remember, that they have lifted up their hands against us.

CHAP. XLVII.

1 I declare to you ye righteous, that the angels record your goodness before the glory of the mighty One in heaven.

2 Wait with patient hope, for formerly you have been injured with calamity and affliction, but now you shall shine like the lights of heaven, and you shall be seen, and the gates of heaven for you shall be opened, your cries have cried for

judgment, and to you it will appear, for an account of all your sufferings, shall be required from the princes, and from all those who assisted those who robbed you.

3 Wait with patience, and always retain your hope, for you shall have great joy, like that of the angels in heaven, and that which shall he done by you shall not be concealed in the day of the great judgment, for you will not be found like sinners, and eternal condemnation shall be far from you in every generation of the world.

4 And now fear not ye righteous, when ye see sinners strong and prosperous in their ways.

5 Be not companions with them, but keep yourselves far from their oppression, be you companions of the host of heaven. You ye sinners say, That all our sins will not be found out, they will not be recorded, but all your sins shall be recorded every day.

6 And now I shew you, that light and darkness, day and night, behold all your sins. Be not impious in your thoughts, lie not, give not up the word of perfection, speak nothing false of the word of the holy and mighty One, praise not your idols, for all your sin, and all your impiety is not for righteousness, but for great wickedness.

7 And now I will shew this mystery. Many sinners shall pervert and transgress against the word of perfection.

8 They shall speak wicked words and lies, perform great works, and shall write books in their own words, but when they shall write all my words correctly in their own languages,

9 They shall neither change nor diminish from my words, but shall write them all correctly, all which from the first I have communicated unto them.

10 And I will shew you another mystery, To the righteous and the wise, there shall be given books of joy, of integrity, and of great wisdom, and to them

shall books be given in which they shall all believe.

11 And over them they shall rejoice, and all the righteous shall be rewarded, who from these shall learn to know the way of righteousness.

12 In those days saith the Lord, they shall call, and make the children of the earth to hear their wisdom, and shew them that you are their leaders.

13 And that there shall he a reward over the whole earth, for I and my Son will he united with them for ever in the way of righteousness in their lives. And for you there shall be peace. Rejoice children of righteousness in the truth.

CHAP. XLVIII.

1 After some time my son Mathusala took a wife for his son Lamech.

2 She became pregnant by him, and brought forth a child, whose flesh was white as snow, and red as a rose, and the hair of his head white like wool to its top, and his eyes were beautiful, and when he opened them he enlightened all the house like the sun, the whole house was light.

3 And when he was taken from the hand of the midwife, he opened his mouth and spoke to the Lord of righteousness. Then his father Lamech was afraid of him, and fled away, and came to his own father Mathusala, and said to him, I have begotten a son of a different appearance, he is not like men, but like the angels the children of heaven; for his nature is different, and he is not as we are.

4 His eyes are as the rays of the sun, his countenance glorious, and he appears as if he were not from me, but is like the angels.

5 I am afraid that something wonderful will in his day be done on earth.

6 And now my father, I entreat and request of you to go to our father Enoch, and to hear from him the truth, for his dwelling is with the angels.

7 When Mathusala heard the words of his son, he came to me at the ends of the earth, for he had heard that I was there, and he cried out.

8 I heard his voice, and went to him, saying, Behold, I am here, my son, since thou art come to me.

9 He answered me, and said, On account of a great concern, I am come to thee, and by reason of a difficult sight, I have come near to thee.

10 And now my father hear me, for to my son Lamech a child has been born, whose resemblance is not like him, and whose nature is not like the nature of men. His colour is whiter than snow, and redder than the rose, the hairs of his head are whiter than white wool, his eyes like the rays of the sun, and when he opened them, he enlightened the whole house.

11 And when he was taken from the hand of the midwife, he opened his mouth, and praised the Lord of heaven.

12 His father Lamech feared, and fled to me, and believed the child not to be from him, but he thought he was like the angels of heaven, and behold, I am come to thee, that thou mightest shew the truth.

13 Then I, Enoch, answered, and said, The Lord will perform a new work upon the earth, and this I have explained, and seen in a vision: I have declared to thee, that in the time of the companions of my father Jared, those who were from the height of heaven transgressed the commandment of the Lord; behold, they committed sins, and laid aside their order, and mingled with women, with them they transgressed, married with them, and begot children.

14 Therefore there shall be a great destruction upon all the earth, a flood, a great destruction shall be in one year.

15 This child who is born to you shall remain upon the earth, and his three sons shall be saved with him, for when all mankind who are upon the earth shall die, he shall be secure.

16 And his posterity upon the earth shall beget giants, not spiritual, but carnal, and there shall be a great punishment upon the earth, and it shall be washed from all corruption. And now inform thy son Lamech, that he who is born is his child in truth, and he shall call his name Noah, for he shall be to you a survivor, and he and his children shall be secure from the corruption which shall come upon the earth, from all the sin and from all the wickedness, which shall be accomplished on the earth in his days. After that there shall be greater wickedness, than that which was first accomplished, on the earth, for I know

the secrets of the holy One, because the Lord himself has revealed and declared them to me, and of them I have read in the tablets of heaven.

17 And upon them I saw it written, that generation after generation shall offend, until a righteous race shall arise, until offences and crime shall perish, and pass away, from off the earth, and all goodness shall come upon it.

18 And now my son, inform thy son Lamech,

19 That the child who is born is his child in truth, and that there is no deceit

20 When Mathusala heard the words of his father Enoch, who had shewn him every thing which was concealed, he departed with seeing, and called the

name of that child Noah, because he was to restore the earth after its total destruction.

21 Another book which Enoch wrote for his son Mathusala, and for those who should come after him, and preserve their state of life in the latter days. You who have laboured shall wait in those days until the workers of wickedness be destroyed, and the power of the guilty pass away. Wait until sin shall vanish away, for their names shall be blotted out of the books of the holy One, their seed shall be destroyed for ever, and their spirits slain, they shall cry out, and lament in the place of misery, where they cannot see, and they shall burn in the fire where there is no earth. There I saw as it were a cloud which could not seen through, for by reason of the depth of it I was not able to behold its height. I saw a flame of fire burning brightly, and as it were splendid mountains whirled around and shaken hither and thither.

22 And I asked one of the holy angels who was with me, and said, What is this splendid object, for it is not heaven but a flame of fire which burns, and there is the voice of the cries of weeping, of lamentation, and of great torment.

23 And he said to me, In that place which thou seest, there the spirits of sinners and blasphemers shall be thrust, of those who shall do evil, and of those who shall pervert all which the Almighty has spoken by the mouth of the prophets, all which they ought to do; for concerning these things there shall be

writings and books above in heaven, that the angels may read them, and know what shall be done both to sinners, and to the spirits of the humble, to those who have suffered in their flesh, but been rewarded by God, and of those who have been insulted by wicked men, who have loved God, who have been attached neither to gold, or silver, or to any good thing in the world, but have given their bodies to affliction,

24 To those who from the time of their birth have not desired the riches of the earth, but have regarded themselves as a breath which passes away.

25 And this they have observed, and much the Lord has proved them, and their spirits have been found in purity, that they might praise his name. I have related all their blessings in a book, and the mighty One has rewarded them, for they have been found to love heaven with an aspiration for ever. God has said, While they have been trodden down by wicked men, they have heard from them invectives and blasphemies, and they have been insulted while they were praising me, and now I will call the spirits of the good from the generation of light, and will change those who have been born in darkness, who in their bodies have not received the honour which their faith deserved.

26 I will bring them into the splendid light of those who love my holy, and I will place each of them on a throne of glory, of glory his own, and they shall be exalted for times without number. For the judgment of God is righteousness.

27 For he will give faith to the faithful in the habitations of upright ways, and they shall see that those who are born in darkness shall be cast into darkness, while the righteous shall be exalted, sinners when they behold them shall cry out, while they exist in splendour, and proceed on to the days and times which before for them had been written.

Here ends the vision of Enoch the prophet. May the benediction of his prayer, and the gift of his appointed time, be with his beloved. Amen.

Notes.

CHAP. I.

Verse **4,** See this prophecy fulfilled, Exodus, xix. 18.

Verse **6,** See this prophecy fulfilled, Genesis, vii. 20.

Verse **9,** This is quoted by St. Jude the apostle, verses 14, and 15 of his Epistle, and it is a certain proof that the Book of Enoch is the work of him whose name it bears.

CHAP. II.

*Verse*s **2, 10,** That the angels took wives, is proved to be true by Moses; the names of the two chief leaders are proved by Jonathan ben Uzziel, and the wickedness of those times by the Testament of Reuben, and the punishment of the angels for the crime which they had committed, is proved by St. Peter, and St. Jude, as will be seen in the note on chapter iv. 6, 15. Now it is shewn by Moses in Genesis, vi. 2, 4, That the sons of God saw the daughters of men that they were fair, and they took them wives of all which they chose. There were giants in the earth in those days, and also after that when the sons of God came in unto the daughters of men, and they bare children to them, the same became mighty men, who were of old men of renown. Now, the sons of God described by Moses, cannot be made into the sons of men, for he has particularly pointed out what they really were, and the sons of God described by Moses, by the Seventy have been translated angels, for the phrase in Hebrew is precisely the same with sons of God, or angels, Job, i. 6, and the mighty and men of renown mentioned by Moses, Genesis, vi. 4, were the children of the sons of God or angels, which agrees with the description of Enoch, chapter ii. 11, and the giants mentioned in Genesis, vi. 4, in Hebrew are called Nephilim, which word signifies fallen, because a part of their heavenly power was fallen, and they were nearer to the nature of men, more of an earthly nature, and not of such great power as the men of renown, which agrees with the description of the second sort of giants mentioned by Enoch, chap. ii. 11, which have also

120

the same name as it is written in the Greek language; and these are clear proofs that Enoch and Moses both described the same wickedness. And Jonathan ben Uzziel, in his Targum on the law distinctly mentions the names of two of the evil angels, who were the principal leaders of others into wickedness. On the expression nephilim, giants, Genesis, vi. 4, he has the following remark, Samiaza and Aziel fell from heaven, and were upon earth in those days, and these are the two complained of by the holy angels in Enoch, chap. iii. b, 6. And it may be seen in the Testament of Reuben, that he said to his sons, Charge your wives and daughters that they trim not their heads, and will them to chasten their looks, for every woman who dealeth deceitfully in these things is reserved unto the punishment of the world to come, for by such means the watchers were deceived who were before the flood, for as soon as they saw them they fell in love one with another, and conceived a working in their minds, and they changed themselves into the shape of men, and appeared unto them in company with their husbands, and the women by conceiving the desire of them in the imagination of their minds brought forth giants, for the watchers appeared unto them of height unto heaven. Now it may be seen that the angels mentioned by Jonathan are the same described by Enoch, chap. iii. 5, 6, and it is shewn by Jonathan, that they were a part of those described by Moses, and the quotation from the Testament of Reuben, though it describes wickedness of a different kind, yet it agrees with the description of Enoch, chap. ii. 14, and with the description of Moses, Genesis, v. 6, and it also proves the truth of the book of Enoch, chap. ix. 18, where it is said, Their wives also shall be judged, who led astray the angels of heaven, that they might salute them. And it may be seen that these proofs taken from the book of Genesis, from the Targum of Jonathan, and from the Testament of Reuben, clearly shew that the wickedness of the angels the sons of heaven, described by Enoch, and the wickedness of the sons of God, described by Moses, are both descriptions of the same wickedness, and that they clearly shew the sins of the angels for which they were bound, as will be seen in the notes on chapter iv. 6, 15. And they who are of opinion that this could not be done, let them try if they can find out any other way that giants of great stature could be produced, for there have been children produced from the different people of many nations of the world, but these children arrive at no greater stature than other people, and the giants spoken of in Numbers, xiii. 33, and other places of Scripture appear to have had their origin as described in the Testament of Reuben in this note, by the appearance of the evil spirits in a gigantic stature, as I can see no other way that is likely, and those nations had dealings with familiar spirits, but the evil angels were bound, so that they could not do what they had done in the time of Enoch, yet they might cause the production of giants in the manner described by Reuben.

Verse 7, I altered this verse by the Greek of Georgius Syncellus, and what I have done is shewn to be right by Chap. xlviii. 16.

Verse 8, The name Armon may be derived from Arar, in Hebrew, he spake evil, or he cursed, swore, which is Ar in Kai, and Min, on, or upon, because they had sworn upon that mountain, or from Aram, he swore them, and On, because, or, for the sake of, because they had sworn upon that mountain, for the sake of the wickedness which they intended to commit, and it may be seen in Buxtorf's Lexicon, that Armon in Hebrew signifies the top of a mountain, and the residence of a famous chief, and in this place it may signify the top of the mount on which the angels swore, and the residence of those famous chiefs when they began their wickedness. And the place where this mount is believed to be, is called the land of Armenia, and the land of Armenia appears to have derived its name from Armen, the third of the leaders of the evil angels, who taught the signs of the earth, and the name of a province or land in Hebrew, composed of the Hebrew letters Aleph and Yod, which affixed to the name Armen compose the name Armenia, and by that name a considerable portion of the land in that part of the world is known, and the land of Armenia is in Hebrew the land of Ararat, (see the Hebrew Bible, and the margin of the Bible, 2 Kings, xix. 37.) and mount Ararat of the Armenians appears to be the mount on which the angels swore, for it appears to be shewn in the book of Enoch, at the end of the seventh chapter, in a part taken from the Chronographia of

Georgius Syncellus, that it had been declared by the Almighty to Enoch, concerning the mount on which the angels swore, that to the end there shall not depart from it cold, and snow, and frost, and dew, and that which descends upon it shall not descend unless to a curse, until the day of the great judgment. Now the top of mount Ararat of the Armenians is always covered with snow, as it had been foretold in the part taken from the Chronographia of Syncellus, and I have read in the Church of England Magazine, and many other books, that no person was able to ascend to the top of mount Ararat of the Armenians, which shews the effects of the curse of the Almighty on all who should descend thereon, and that there may be no mistake concerning words, it must be evident, that the curse which was foretold would be upon all who came upon the mountain, for the feet of the people who came upon it would always be descending upon it, at the same time that they were ascending or climbing higher upon the mountain. And the name Ararat may also be derived from the Hebrew Arar, he spake evil, or he cursed, swore; and At, a juggler, deceiver, or deceit, whence the meaning of the name would be, the cursed deceiver, or the cursed deceit; a name very properly applied to the mountain where the deceiver first descended, and the cursed deceit was begun. And as mount Ararat has been cursed by the Almighty on account of the cursed deceit and wickedness which was there begun upon the earth, so for that reason the name cursed deceit, the meaning of the name Ararat in Hebrew, is also very properly applied to that mountain, for it is a standing witness of the curse of the Almighty upon it, because people have ascended to the top of higher mountains than it, with far less difficulty than there has been in ascending only a small part of the height of mount Ararat. But it may be observed that the ark of Noah rested on the mountains of Ararat, but as there are more mountains than one called Ararat, and Noah was under the direction of the Almighty, his ark would not be suffered to rest on that mountain, on which all was cursed that descended. Now to shew this in a shorter way, it may be seen that Armon can be derived from Ar and Min, or from Aram and On, because the angels had sworn upon that mountain, that it also signifies the top of a mount, and the residence of a chief, that it appears to be in the land of Armenia—that Armenia appears to be derived from the third of the leaders of the evil angels, and the name of a province in Hebrew—that it also might be derived from the name Armon, &c.—that the land of Armenia is in Hebrew the land of Ararat—that Mount Ararat appears to be mount of which Armon signified the top—that the name Ararat can be derived from Arar, he cursed, and At, a deceiver, or deceit, because upon it the angels swore to execute their deceit. And it may also be derived from the curse of the Almighty upon that deceit And these words all agree so well with the words from which they are derived, both in letters and meaning, that to me they clearly shew the mount on which the angels swore, to be mount Ararat. And these names may be derived otherwise than I have here shewn, for Armon may be derived from Aram he swore them, and On, often added to the ends of words, which might signify the swearing. And Ararat might be derived from Arar he cursed, swore, and Hat sin, which would signify the cursed sin, that is the sin causing that curse the deluge, which name clearly shews the truth.

If it should he observed that it is not clearly shewn in the part taken from the Chronographia of Syncellus, that it was the Almighty who had declared, that there would be a curse upon the mount on which the angels swore, it may be answered, that Syncellus declares he has taken all from the first book of Enoch concerning the watchers, and this will shew that it is put in the right place at the end of the seventh chapter, where the Almighty had declared to Enoch the punishment of the watchers, and these words from Syncellus are such as could be spoken by none but the Almighty, or one sent by him, for the effects of the curse remain upon mount Ararat, so that no person is able to ascend to the top of it, and this clearly shews that the curse foretold in the fragment of Syncellus could proceed from no other but the Almighty.

Verse 9, From the beginning of this verse to the end of the first verse of the next chapter, is altered by the Greek fragment of the book of Enoch in the Chronographia of Syncellus, which was far more correct, and several of the names of the evil angels are altered, for I saw that the names in this chapter, and the names in chapter xxv. 2, and in the Greek of Syncellus, were the same, if they were corrected, I wrote them all down opposite each other, and numbered them, and I found that the second name in the second chapter should be divided in two, and that the name Tumael should be made the 17th and that the remaining three should be the 18th, 19th, 20th, and I saw that in chapter xxv. the 13th name should be the 14th, and the 14th the 13th, and that the 15th should be taken out, because it appears to be the same as the 19th, in the way they stood before I altered them, and that name which was the 16th became the 15th and the remaining five became the 16th, 17th, 18th, 19th, 20th. Then I saw by comparing them one with another, that they were all intended for the same names, though there be variations in the spelling, and the names are taken either from the names, which were in this chapter, or in the 25th chapter, or from the Greek of Syncellus, and I took the names which had been most commonly used, or those least like one another.

As Hoffmann has shewn what he supposes to be the derivations of the names of the evil angels, I shall also attempt to do the same: but as they were then evil angels, I am of opinion that their names cannot be derived from any thing that is good.

1   Samiaza, a powerful name.
2   Arstikapha, he swore to the determination.
3   Armen, from the oath.
4   Akibeel, the oath of the ruler.
5   Tarniel, wonderful strength.
6   Ramiel, exalted strength.
7   Danial, the strong judge.
8   Zakiel, great power.
9   Barakel, strong lightning.
10 Azaziel, very strong power.
11 Anners, the oath of the ruler.
12 Bataryal, the strong lion.
13 Ananel, a strong cloud.
14 Thausael, the powerful commanded sign.
15 Samiel, the strong name.

16   Ertael, the oath of the mount.
17   Tumael, astonishing strength.
18   Tarel, strong labour.
19   Yomyael, it was done that day.
20   Sariel, strongly bound.

Verse **11,** The giants have been mentioned in the note on verse 2, but the accounts of the origin of the giants, and the battle of the giants in ancient authors, appear to have been taken from the books of Enoch, and Moses, or from some others which gave a part of the same description, for this 11th verse of this 2nd chapter of Enoch, and the 4th verse of the 6th chapter of Genesis, shew the origin of the giants, and the description in the Pantheon, which is partly taken from the Theogony of Hesiod, appears to be like them, viz.: The giants were the sons of Terra, (the earth) when she was impregnated with the blood of Caelum, (heaven) which flowed from that dishonourable wound given him by his son Saturn. Now it is known by them who are acquainted with Hebrew, that the word Adam signifies earth, and the daughters of men, Genesis vi. 2, are in the Hebrew daughters of Adam, which shews they were earth, and the sons of God described in Genesis, vi. 2, or angels the sons of heaven in Enoch, ii. 2, who descended from heaven, and caused the production of the giants, clearly shew that earth, (the daughters of men) was impregnated with the blood of heaven, (the sons of God, or angels whose dwelling was in heaven) but, according to the Pantheon, that blood flowed from that dishonourable wound given him by his son Saturn. Now according to the philosophical meaning of the word Saturn in the Pantheon, it signifies Time. So in Time, after a considerable number of years were expired, in the days of Jared, the angels the sons of heaven were deceived, as may be seen in chap. xxv. 4, and caused the production of the giants, which shews the dishonourable wound given by Saturn or Time. And it may be seen in the book of Enoch, in chap. iv. 13 and xxxv. 30, that there had been a battle of the giants, for the giants, the children of fornication, the offspring of the watchers, mentioned in Enoch, iv. 13, are the great giants, the Nephilim, and Elioud in Enoch, ii. 11, and the elephants, camels, and asses in Enoch xxxv. 30, are the same, and these places clearly shew that there had been a battle with the giants, And it is likely that the evil angels were the Titans, and that the great giants were the sons of those evil angels or Titans, for in Hesiod's Theogony they are called the host of glorious Titans, and in another part there is the expression, gods encountering gods, and in Virgil, Eneid 6th, 725, they are called Titan stars, and from these expressions, it appears to be likely that the evil angels called Titans, also fought in the battles of the giants, and according to Hesiod they were defeated by Jupiter and bound in the west, but in truth they were taken from their wickedness by the command of the Almighty and bound in the west, for the wickedness which they taught on earth, which was certainly warring against the Almighty Ruler of earth and heaven.

Verses **11,12.** These were corrupted by the Jews, they are now corrected.

Verses **20, 21, 22,** These verses were taken out, the 21st was taken out to hinder it to be discovered that the land of Armenia received its name, because it was the land where Armen the third of the leaders of the evil angels taught the signs of the earth, that the prophecy at the end of the seventh chapter might not be discovered.

CHAP. III.

Verse **1** is altered by the Greek of Syncellus, which was more correct.

Verses **2 and 7,** are altered by the Greek of Syncellus, by which they are made more correct.

Verses **6, 15,** These are proved to be true both by St. Peter, and St. Jude, (see 2 Peter ii 4, and Jude 6) and these verses in their epistles appear to have been taken in a contracted form out of the book of Enoch, and what they have taken clearly shews the punishment of the angels for the wickedness which they had taught, as may be seen in chap. iii. 5, and they also shew that the book of Enoch is truth.

Verse **13** This clearly shews that there had been a battle of the giants, see note on Chap. ii 11.

Verse **15,** This is altered by the Greek of Syncellus, and shewn to be right by chap. xxxv. 29.

Verse **15,** Bind them for 70 generations &c. Now the 70 generations can only be taken from the time of the flood of Noah, when all their sons would be slain, because it is shewn in chapter ii. 10, that they continued in their madness until the flood, which was in the year 1655 from the creation of the world. Now if the time of a generation be taken at 70 years, according to the description of Moses in the 10th verse of the 90 Psalm, it will be 70X 70=4900+1655=6555, there will be 4900 years from the time that the angels were bound, and 6555 years from the creation, to a little past the middle of the time when the judgment is expected to be, for it is believed that it will begin about the year of the world 6000, and continue a thousand years. But the Jewish year consisted only of 360 days, and as that way of computing time would continue among the Jews till the destruction of Jerusalem, there would be 4074 years from the creation to that time, in which every year would want 5 days of the time of the earth's revolution. Now 4074 X 5= 20370−365 =55 years 295 days, to be taken from the present calculation of time, and if 55 years be taken from the present calculation, there will remain 6500 years from the creation to that time, which is believed to be in the middle of the time of the great judgment. This is certainly very remarkable, and a more particular description of the time of the great judgment will be found in the note on chap. xli. 19.

CHAP. V.

Verse **5,** Ireneus in the second century distinctly alluded to the embassy of Enoch to the angels. He said, But also Enoch, whether of the circumcision pleasing God when he was a man, was sent an embassy to the angels, and was translated, and kept till now a witness of the just judgment of God, because the angels who transgressed fell into condemnation, but the man pleasing to God is taken to happiness.

CHAP. VI.

Verse **18,** I altered a word and what I have done is shewn to be right by chap. ix. 10.

Verses **21, 22,** This description is extremely beautiful.

CHAP. VII.

Verse **8,** This shews that the spirits of the giants shall dwell on earth.

Verse **9,** Evil spirits are like clouds, as Enoch said of the spirits of the giants.

Verse **11,** Partof this verse is taken from the Greek fragment of Syncellus.

Verse **16,** This part was taken out of the Book of Enoch, that the mount might not be known, or the curse which was foretold to remain upon it, because they would prove the book of Enoch to be truth, but it is now restored from the Chronographia of Syncellus, who has declared that he has taken all from the first book of Enoch concerning the watchers, and this follows the part which he had extracted before, and clearly shews itself to be the sentence of the Almighty upon that mountain, as the part before shews the sentence or judgment of the watchers, and the truth of this prophecy is clearly shewn by mount Ararat, as may be seen in the note on chapter ii. 8. And it is likely that Syncellus has made these extracts from some uncorrupted copy, for the purpose of shewing the truth of these parts of the book of Enoch which had been corrupted, for there are other parts corrected from the fragment of Syncellus, of which every particular has not been mentioned.

CHAP. VIII.

Verse **7,** It is believed by Hoffmann that Ikisat is the throne of the Almighty.

Verse **7,** It appears to be a certainty from chapter xxxix. 44, 45 and other places, that there were seven of those watchers, and in

Tobit xii. 15, Raphael declared that he was one of the seven angels, and they also appear to be the same mentioned in Rev. iv. 5, and in Zachariah iv. 10, and it is very likely that the seventh will be Phanuel, whose description in chapter xiii. 9, I have inserted in the book and their names may perhaps be more easily remembered in the following lines, Michael, Gabriel, Raphael, Phanuel, Sarakiel, and Uriel, and also Raguel.

CHAP. IX.

Verse **1,** It is clearly shewn by philosophy that the wind is the air in motion, and it is evident that the greatest part of the ornaments of creation in this world are in the air, and that the earth is kept in its orbit by the pressure of the air, which was justly called attraction by the great Sir Isaac Newton.

Verse **3,** This clearly shews the power of attraction, which is in the air.

Verse **5,** And it is the same power of attraction in the air which sustain the heavens, being there placed by the decree of the Almighty, see chap. xxv. 24, 25, 26, 27, 28, 29.

Verses **14, 15, 16,** These angels had fallen before those who descended upon mount Armon, because these last might not be bound until the flood of Noah, when all their sons would be slain, chap. iv. 15, and that would be after the time when Enoch was taken to heaven.

Verse **18,** Their wives &c. This is shewn to be true by the Testament of Reuben in the note on chap. 2, 10, where it is shewn that he said, Charge your wives and daughters that they trim not their heads and will them to chasten their looks for by such means the watchers were deceived which were before the flood.

Verse **22,** These are also angels who fell before the watchers, see the note on verses 14,15,16.

CHAP. X.

Verse **7,** This shews that the spirit of Abel accused Cain, which is proved by Genesis iv. 10, when the Almighty said to Cain, The voice of thy brother's blood crieth unto me from the ground. Now the voice of the blood of Abel could be nothing but the spirit of Abel. See **Chap.** iii 10, 11.

Verses **9,10,** This shews that the spirits of the dead are divided by a gulf, and it is proved by Luke xvi. 26, when Abraham said to the rich man, Between us and you there is a great gulf fixed. This is a very clear proof of the truth of the book of Enoch, because there is nothing like this in any other part of scripture, except these words of our Saviour by which it is proved.

Verse 12, This shews the punishment of the dead immediately after death, and it is proved in Luke xvi. 23, by our blessed Saviour, who said of the rich man, In hell he lifted up his eyes, being in torments. This also clearly shews the truth of the book of Enoch, and there is nothing like it in the Old Testament.

Verse 14, This shews that the souls of the wicked will not be destroyed at the judgment.

Verse 29, For towards the north &c. This is proved by scripture to be a prophecy of our blessed Saviour, and the holy place here spoken of is Jerusalem, and it may be seen by the map of the world, that Jerusalem is on the northside of the equinoctial, and it is shewn in Psalm xlviii. 2, that the city of the great king was on the sides of the north, and the life which was to be planted in the holy place, was our blessed Saviour, for it may be seen in John ii. 25, that our Saviour said, 1 am the resurrection and the life, and in John xiv. 6, that he said, I am the way, and the truth, and the life. And it is shewn in Matthew, iv. 5, that Jerusalem was the holy city, where our Saviour was planted, for he called the temple his Father's house, John ii. 16, and his house, Luke xix. 46, and he taught daily in the temple, Luke, xix, 47, and that Jerusalem was towards the habitation of the everlasting King, is shewn 2 Kings, xxiii. 27, when the Almighty said, I will remove Judah out of my sight. Now these places clearly shew that towards the north (in Jerusalem) life (our Saviour) was planted in the holy place, (in Jerusalem) towards the habitation of the everlasting King. And it also appears to be shewn that the place appointed, for the saints after the resurrection will be towards the north, for it is shewn by Enoch, chap. xx. 1, 2, that angels went towards the north to measure, and in verse 7, the resurrection is foretold, and in chap. xxvi. 5, it is shewn, that between the north and the west, the angels received their ropes to measure out a place for the elect and the righteous. And in Isaiah, xiv. 13, it is said of the king of Babylon, Thou hast said in thy heart, I will ascend into heaven, I will sit upon the mount of the congregation in the sides of the north, I shall be like the Most High. Now it is shewn by these places of Scripture that the place appointed for the righteous will be on the north, and that in Revelation, xxi. 10, it was called the holy Jerusalem, and that it appears to be shewn by 2 Kings, xxiii. 27, that it was not far distant from the terrestrial Jerusalem.

CHAP. XI.

Verse **4,** The valley of the son of Hinnom according to Hoffmann, see note, chapter xxxix. 48.

Verse **12.** These might be called trees of judgment, because the frankincense was used in offerings, perhaps these might be offered, that the judgments of the Almighty might not come upon them.

Verse **17,** Neketro appears to be derived from the Hebrew word Katar, a perfume, or incense (Numbers xvi. 46,) which was used in sacrifice to the Almighty, which word in Niphal is Niktar, from which the word Nectar is derived. Sarira appears to be derived from the Hebrew word Tzari, which signifies the juice of the balm tree, which is of great value. It is called balm, Genesis, xxxvii. 25, and Jeremiah, U. 8. Kalboneba appears to be derived from the Hebrew Chelbonah, which is translated galbanum, Exodus, xxx. 24, audit is called a resin in Buxtorf's Lexicon. Now this water which flowed like Neketro or nectar might have these names from different nations.

Verse **26,** The revolutions of the luminaries are shewn at chap xxvii.

CHAP. XII.

Verse 1, This shews that they who were before Enoch thought it good to speak, and God has spoken by the mouth of his prophets, (Chap. xlviii. 23,) and it is proved by Luke, i. 70, where it is shewn, That God spake by the mouth of his holy prophets which have been since the world began, and it is also proved Acts, iii. 21, and Romans, xv. 4, and 1 Timothy, iii. 16, and these proofs clearly shew that from the beginning of the world there had been holy prophets, and that Enoch was one of these holy prophets.

Verse 3, Here I corrected a mistake, or a part corrupted, as may be seen by this book, chap. xxv. 42.

CHAP. XIII.

Verse **19,** Here Enoch shews that the Almighty called the stars by their names, and in chap. xxv. 30, where he calls their names they answer him for ever and ever. There are places like these in scripture, see Job, xxxviii. 35, Psalm, cxlvii. 4, Isaiah, xl. 26, Baruch, iii. 34. But in the latter part of this 19th verse, Enoch says that their conversion was into the number of the angels, and of the faithful. Now in Daniel, viii. 10, when he saw in a vision the wickedness of Antiochus Epiphanes, under the emblem of a horn, he says, it cast some of the host of heaven, and of the stars to the ground, by which it was shewn that he would destroy the mighty and the holy people, Daniel, viii. 24, and in Daniel, xii. 3, it may be seen that they who turn many to righteousness shall shine as the stars. Now this description of Enoch agrees with other parts of Scripture, for when they shall shine as the stars, they may also be called stars. And it may also be seen in Deut., iv. 19, and many other places of Scripture, that the stars are in Hebrew called Tzaba, which signifies a host or army, in the plural Tzabaoth, which shews that these descriptions of Enoch and Moses are to the same purpose. But it is believed by some that the fixed stars are so many suns, enlightening other orbs, peopled with a race of intelligent beings, who like us are children of dust, and heirs of immortality, and in the year 1798, there were 75 millions of these stars discovered in a very small space of the heavens, and it is also believed that there are so many of these stars yet undiscovered, that it would be impossible to number them all. Now all that innumerable quantity of stars give a wonderful' idea of the power of the great Almighty Maker; and if these stars be all attended by planets, it will certainly be more wonderful. And as it may be clearly seen by reading the Scriptures, that every being to whom an immortal soul was given, might have had a certainty of obtaining everlasting life, which was prepared for mankind by the God supreme. Therefore it may be seen, that if all the innumerable army of planets were inhabited by human beings having immortal souls, yet if their bodies were made of terrestrial matter, they would undoubtedly fall like the first inhabitants of the earth, and be for ever lost without a Saviour to suffer death for them, and as all the days since the time of the creation to the beginning of the day of the great judgment, that is, the days of 6000 years, would be insufficient to teach them, and to suffer for them all, for our blessed Saviour was upon this earth for 33 years and a half. Therefore for any being of divine nature to suffer for them all appears to be an impossibility, and it also appears to be an impossibility that beings made of terrestrial matter could keep themselves entirely free from sin. Therefore it appears to be a certain fact, that there can be no beings made terrestrial matter dwelling on the planetary orbs, and that if there be inhabitants on these orbs, they must be of a celestial origin, and what Enoch said will be found to be truth, that the conversion of the stars will be into the number of the angels, and of the faithful. And it has also been said, that this earth will appear as a planet to the inhabitants of other planets, but that is clearly shewn to be impossible, because when people ascend in a balloon, they often arise to that height, that they cannot see the earth, which is a certain proof that the earth would be invisible to the inhabitants of the planets, if these inhabitants were made of terrestrial matter like the people of the earth.

CHAP. XIV.

Verse **3,** This is a remarkable and particular prophecy of our blessed Saviour, shewing that he shall sit on the throne of his glory, which may be seen in five places in this book, in which our Saviour is called the elect One, the same name by which he is also called by the prophet Isaiah, in chap. xlii. 1. And in one place our Saviour is called the son of woman, and this prophecy has been proved to be true by our blessed Saviour himself in Matthew xxv. 30. Now this proves the truth of the prophesies of Enoch.

Verse **6,** This part, his countenance was full of grace, is proved in the gospel by St. John chap. i. 14, But the latter part of this verse, and other places in this book are remarkable predictions of our blessed Saviour, for there are twelve places in this book where our blessed Saviour is called the Son of man,, and the angels have shewn the great power and goodness of the Son of man to righteous Enoch. Now the power and goodness of the Son of man have been clearly shewn in the gospel by St. Matthew to many nations, and our Saviour has more than thirty times called himself the Son of man, as may be seen in that gospel. Now any of these twelve places in this book proved by our blessed Saviour himself might be sufficient to shew the truth of the prophecies of Enoch, but twelve places in the book of Enoch proved by thirty-two places in the gospel by St. Matthew, are stronger proofs than are often found respecting any ancient author, and they clearly prove that Enoch was a true prophet of the most high God, and that this is his book.

Verse 7, The first part of this verse, The son of man to whom righteousness belongs, is proved, John, viii. 46, when our Saviour said to the Jews, Which of you convinceth me of sin; but the latter part of this verse, Who will reveal all the treasures of that which is concealed, is a very remarkable prophecy of our blessed Saviour by Enoch. I have looked in vain for the Scripture from which it might be taken, but I soon discovered it in the book of Enoch the righteous, and the proof of it was spoken by the woman of Samaria, John iv. 25, when she said, I know that Messias cometh, who is called Christ, when he is come, he will tell us all things, and our Saviour confirmed the truth of what she spoke, by saying, I that speak unto thee am he. This clearly shews the book of Enoch to be truth.

Verse 13, This is proved by Rev. vi. 9, 10, The souls of them that were slain cried with a loud voice, saying, How long, O Lord, holy and true, dost thou not judge, and avenge our blood on them that dwell on the earth. This also proves the truth of the prophecies of Enoch.

Verse 14, This is proved by St, John, Rev. xx. 12, And I saw the dead small and great stand before God, and the books were opened, and another book was opened, which is the book of life. There is also a book mentioned in Psalm, Lxix, 28 called the book of the living, but in all the books of the Old Testament, there is no description of any person who saw the book of life opened, except Enoch the righteous, or in the New Testament, except St

John the divine. This is another proof of the truth of the book of Enoch.

CHAP. XV.

Verse 1, The fountain of righteousness and springs of wisdom appear to be like the operations of the holy spirit, and many expressions of holy Scripture are to the same purpose, for it may be seen in Job, xxviii. 28, That the fear of the Lord is wisdom, and in Prov. xiv. 27, That the fear of the Lord is a fountain of life, and in Prov. xvii. 22, That understanding is a well spring of life. So by these it is shewn, that wisdom and understanding are fountains of life. And it may be seen in Prov. xviii. 4, That the well spring of wisdom is a flowing brook; and in the Wisdom of Solomon, chap. vii. 22, That wisdom is an understanding spirit, holy; and in verse 25, That wisdom is the breath of the power of God, and a pure influence or stream flowing from the glory of the Almighty; and in Ecclus. xxiv. 30,31, it is said, That wisdom came as a brook, and the brook became a river, and the river a sea. And David said to the Almighty, Psalm, xxxvi. 8, 9, You shall make me drink of the river of your pleasures, for with you is the fountain of life; and in Jeremiah, ii. 13, and xvii. 13, the Almighty is called the fountain of living waters, also, see Isaiah, xxxv. 6, 7, and xli. 18, and xliv. 3, and li. 1, &c., &c. And here is another place which would easily be brought to remembrance by the Jews, because there was a command from King Ahasuerus that they were all to be destroyed. This place is in Esther, xi. 10, For then the Jews cried unto God, and from their cry, as it were from a little fountain, was made a great flood, (or river) even much water. Now some of these places of Scripture would be brought to remembrance by the people, when our Saviour said, If any man thirst, let him come to me, and drink. He that believeth on me as the Scripture hath said, out of his belly shall flow rivers of living water, John vii. 37, 38, And some of the people said, This is the Christ. Now the first and second verses of this chapter of Enoch appear to me to be the Scripture to which our Saviour referred, for those who were thirsty had their habitations with the Elect and holy One, (our Saviour) the thirsty drank, and were filled with wisdom. In that hour this Son of man was invoked &c. Now this invoking or calling upon the Elect One (our Saviour) was the flowing of wisdom or living water. Yet though all these expressions, a fountain of righteousness, springs of wisdom, a fountain or well of life, a fountain of living waters, &c. all signify the operations of the holy Spirit, yet in different people there are different operations from the same Spirit, as may be seen in 1 Corinthians, xii. 7,8,9,10,11.

Verse **3,** This is a remarkable prophecy of our Saviour, shewing that he would be a support for the righteous and holy to lean upon without failing, which is proved, John vi. 47, when our Saviour said to the Jews, He that believeth on me hath everlasting life. This is also proved, John, xi. 26, and these places of Scripture prove the truth of the book of Enoch. Here are several prophecies of our blessed Saviour near one place in the book of Enoch, but the proofs being in different parts of Scripture caused me to divide them.

Verse **3,** This shews that our Saviour would be the light of nations, which is proved, John, viii. 12, and ix. 5, when our Saviour said, I am the light of the world. The same was also foretold by Isaiah, chap. xlii. 6, but the prophecy of Enoch was long before that. This is what our Saviour has several times declared himself to be, which clearly shews that the book of Enoch is truth.

Verse **4,** This in which Enoch foretold that our Saviour would be the hope of those whose hearts are in trouble, is proved, Mat. xi. 28, when our Saviour said, Come unto me all ye that labour and are heavy laden, and I will give you rest.

Verse **4,** This in which Enoch foretold that all who dwell on earth shall worship before our Saviour, is proved, Phil. ii. 10, where St. Paul declares, That at the name of Jesus every knee shall bow. The same was also foretold by Isaiah, chap. xlv. 25, but it is not there shewn to be a prophecy of our Saviour, as it is in the book of Enoch.

Verse **5,** Here Enoch shews that our Saviour existed in the presence of the Almighty before the world was created, which is proved, John, i. 1, In the beginning was the Word, and the Word was with God, and the Word was God. This is very remarkable, and it clearly shews that many of the mysteries of heaven had been revealed to Enoch the righteous.

Verse 7, Here Enoch shews that in the name of the Saviour people shall be saved, which is proved by Acts, iv. 12, For there is no other name (but Jesus) under heaven given amongst men whereby we may be saved. It is also proved, John, iii. 36, and Rom. x. 13. And it was foretold by the prophet Joel, chap. ii. 32, but it is not by him shewn to be a prophecy of our blessed Saviour, as it is in the book of Enoch the righteous.

Verse 14, This shews that the spirits of those who sleep in righteousness are with the elect One (our Saviour) which is proved by Luke, xxiii. 43, when our Saviour said to the penitent thief, To day shalt thou be with me in paradise. This is another proof of the truth of the prophecies of Enoch.

Verse 20, This shews that the earth shall give up the dead, and it is proved by John, v. 28, 29, when our Saviour said, All that are in the graves shall hear his voice (the voice of the Son of God) and shall come forth, they that have done good unto the resurrection of life, and they that have done evil unto the resurrection of damnation. There is a prophecy of nearly the same meaning in Dan. xii. 2, but the prophecy of Enoch was long before that. This is another proof of the truth of the prophecies of Enoch.

Verse 23, This is a very remarkable prophecy of Enoch shewing that all the righteous shall become angels in heaven, which is proved by Matthew, xxii. 30. And when the Sadducees described the woman to our Saviour, who had been the wife of every one of seven brethren, our Saviour said, Ye do err, not knowing the Scriptures, or the power of God, for in the resurrection they neither marry, nor are given in marriage, but are as the angels of God in heaven, Mat. xxii. 29, 30. Now the New Testament was not written at that time, and in all the books of the Old Testament which we now have, the Sadducees could not get that knowledge of Scripture which they had not, but they might get that knowledge in the book of Enoch the righteous where it may be seen in chap. ii. 10, that some angels took wives, and in Chap. xlviii. 13, that they transgressed the word of the Lord, and married, and in chap. xvi. 23, that they became servants of Satan, and in chap. vi. 4, that they were to be bound on earth. So from these places it must be evident that the angels of God in heaven married not. And that the dead shall rise again, and all the righteous shall become angels in heaven is shewn by Enoch chap. xv. 20, 23. Now the book of Enoch gives a description to the same purpose as the words of our Saviour above quoted: And a description to the same purpose is not to be found in all the books of the Old Testament. Therefore it may be seen that our Saviour accounted the book of Enoch to be Scripture, for the Scripture spoken of by our Saviour could be no other book but the book of Enoch, and if there had been others which gave the same description, it is clear that that description had been taken from the book of Enoch, and the Sadducees could not get that knowledge of Scripture which they had not from books where it was not to be found. This is a certain proof of the truth of the book of Enoch.

CHAP. XVI.

Verse 2, All which existed on earth, the mountain of iron, &c. appear to be the same as those described by Noah in Chap. xxiii. 19.

Verse 16, This is a very clear prophecy of the temple at Jerusalem. See the note on chap. xxvi. 23.

CHAP. XVII.

Verses 13, 14,15, 16, This appears to be like a battle of the giants.

CHAP. XVII.

Verse 5, Darkness has vanished away, there shall be light which shall never end. This is proved by Rev. xxi. 25, For there shall be no night there, (in the holy Jerusalem ver. 10.) This also proves the truth of the book of Enoch.

CHAP. XIX.

Verse **1,** It appears to be a certain fact, that the Jews or others have altered the time which Enoch remained on earth in the Bible to bring the book of Enoch into disrepute, for it is said in Gen. v. 23, that all the days of Enoch were 365 years, This should have been 565 years, for it may be seen in the beginning of this chapter, that when Enoch was in the 500th year of his life he saw a vision, and it may he seen in Chap. xxiii. 4, that Enoch and Noah had been together, which could not have been if Enoch had not been more than 365 years on earth, for he would have been taken away before Noah was born. This may perhaps not please some people who will have all the Scriptures to be correct, and the Bible is certainly a most excellent and valuable book, but it is not free from mistakes, for it may be seen in the books of Kings and Chronicles, when the descriptions are about the same things, that there is sometimes a great variation in numbers, see 1 Kings iv. 26, and 2 Chron. ix. 25, also see 1 Kings ix. 28, and 2 Chron. viii 18, also see 2 Kings viii. 17, 26, and 2 Chron. xxi. 20, and xxii. 2, also see 2 Sam. x. 18, and 1 Chron. xix. 18. Now it may be seen in these places that the numbers are not alike, yet I believe that the commandments of the Almighty remain unaltered in the Bible, and these places here mentioned may be mistakes in writing the numbers by persons not well acquainted with Hebrew, but it is clearly shewn by Mat. xxviii 11, 12, 13, that when the watch had declared the resurrection of our blessed Saviour, the chief priests gave them money to deny it, and it is evident by the Septuagint translation of the Scriptures, that the Jews have taken some parts from the book of Daniel, but the reason of that was shewn in another place. And as Enoch by his prophecies of our blessed Saviour has shewn himself to be a true prophet of the most high God, his descriptions of other things will be found to be truth. And it may be easily seen by examining the book of Enoch that the time of his abode on earth has been altered in the Bible, where it should have been 565 years.

Verse **7,** Two monsters, &c. This clearly means two sorts of monsters, one sort whose name is Leviathan, which is clearly shewn by Job xli. to be the crocodiles or alligators. This sort is also called female, or recipient, as the same word is translated chap. xvi. 27, because these monsters of the deep would receive or take the people when they attempted to save themselves from drowning at the flood.

Verse **8,** And a monster whose name is Behemoth, &c. This word in Hebrew signifies wild beasts, &c. and the Ethiopia word is by Ludolf justly translated tigers, and this sort is called male, or the agent, as the same word is translated chap. xvi. 26, because these monsters of the wilderness at the flood of Noah would drive the people from the mountains into the water, where they would be taken by the monsters of the deep, and as the crocodiles can also live upon the land, they might come out of the water to seize the people, and the punishment of the wicked would then be very great, and it would not end after the earthly body was dead, but their souls would be in misery for ever and ever.

CHAP. XX.

Verse **8,** Here is a beautiful description of the pleasant work of the righteous.

Verses **10,11,** This is a remarkable prophecy of Enoch, shewing that our Saviour shall be the judge, which is proved by John v. 22, when our Saviour said to the Jews, The Father judgeth no man, but hath committed all judgment unto the Son. This clearly shews the book of Enoch to be truth.

CHAP. XXI.

Verse **10,** This is also a remarkable prophecy of our Saviour, shewing that from the beginning the Son of man was concealed or hid, which is proved by Romans, xvi. 25, The preaching of Jesus Christ was kept secret since the world began. This also proves the truth of the book of Enoch.

CHAP. XXII.

Verses **1**, &c., This shews the troubles of the wicked.

CHAP. XXIII.

Verses **19, 20, 21, 22,** It has been shewn at chap. iv. 6, 15, that the evil angels were to be bound and punished, and these verses appear to shew the places of their punishment, for the burning valley in the west appears to be in the Lipari islands, which are west from the Euxine and Caspian seas, (and these seas have been thought to be near the place where Enoch lived) and it is said in history, that there have always been volcanoes in these islands, and these burning mountains appear to be places of punishment, for the Vai di Demona in Sicily has its name from the devils which are believed to be there, but where ever the places of punishment may be, as Enoch has proved himself to be a true prophet of the most high God, his description of the confinement of the angels in those burning valleys will also be right, for the description of our Saviour in Matthew, xxv. 41, is to the same purpose. And perhaps it may be about twenty years since I read in a newspaper of a trial, which was recorded in the law books, which had been just one hundred years before that time, concerning a captain and twenty-four sailors who went on shore on the island of Stromboli, one of the Lipari islands, and they saw a black man driving another man into the burning mountain of Stromboli, and the captain named him, and said, that is such a man from England, and when the sailors came to England, they were told that that man died just at the time they saw him driven into the burning mountain, and the story circulated till it came to the ears of that man's widow who was driven into the burning mountain, and she brought an action at law against the captain for raising such a report. So at the trial the clothes of the man who was dead were brought, and the sailors being all sworn, every one declared the last suit of clothes which that man had worn, appeared to be the clothes which that man had on who was driven into the burning mountain. And the judge said, One, two or three men may be mistaken, but these twenty-four men cannot be all mistaken. So the widow lost her cause. Now this appears to be a certain proof that the burning mountains are places of punishment, but that was clearly shewn before by Enoch. And the Greek word Geene (hell) is derived from the Hebrew Gehinnon, the valley of Hinnon, a place near Jerusalem, and it is shewn in Chap. xxxix. 47, 48, that the wicked among the Jews were to be punished in that place.

Verse 31, In 2 Peter, ii. 5, Noah is called a preacher of righteousness, which might be taken from the following words of Enoch, for the 4th verse of St. Peter's Epistle was taken in a contracted form, from chapter iv. 15, of Enoch, and the following was found in the Greek of Syncellus, and perhaps it is all that now remains of what Noah had said to the wicked people, and it has been spoken one hundred and twenty years before the flood, see Gen. vi. 3, And now I say to you ye sons of men, there is great wrath against you, and against your sons, and this wrath shall never depart from you, until the time of the slaughter of your sons; all your beloved shall perish, and all the mighty shall die from all the earth, for all the days of your lives from this time shall not be more than an hundred and twenty years, and think not that ye shall live any more years, for ye will find no way of escaping the punishment, with which the King of all ages will punish you, so never believe that you shall escape that.

CHAP. XXIV.

Verse 1, This shews the dreadful punishment of the evil angels.

CHAP. XXV.

Verse 2, Here some of the names of the evil angels were altered. See note on chap. ii. 9.

Verse 4, The name Satan is not exactly the same in Ethiopia, but the description here given shews him to be the first, and he who seduced all the angels, which are certain proofs that he is Satan, and a translator should give the right meaning.

Verse **4, 5, and xxvi. 5,** Here some words were transposed, and an ellipsis supplied, and what was done is shewn to be right by chap. vii. 7, and other places of the book.

Verse **19,** In this and several other places the word which before was oath, I have translated decree, and by comparing the 26th and 27th verses of this chapter with Job, xxxviii. 10, and Prov. viii. 29, it will be seen that I use the same word which the translators of the Bible used to express the same meaning, and the word in this chapter appears to be derived from the same root in Hebrew.

Verse **40,** According to their degrees of depravity, they shall be imprisoned. This is proved by Matthew, xi. 24, when our Saviour said, That it shall be more tolerable for the land of Sodom at the day of judgment than for Capernaum. This also proves the truth of the prophecies of Enoch.

CHAP. XXVI.

Verse **19,** This is "sufficient of itself alone," to shew that the book of Enoch is the work of him whose name it bears. It was quoted by St. Paul, Heb. xi. 5, By faith Enoch was translated, that he should not see death, for before he was translated he had this testimony, that he pleased God. It is also quoted by Solomon in his Wisdom, chap. iv. 10, He pleased God. And it is also quoted by Jesus the son of Sirach, Ecclus. xliv. 16, Enoch pleased God, and was translated, being an example of repentance to all generations. And the truth of this is also clearly shewn by Moses, Gen. v. 24, for the Almighty would take none, but those who pleased him. It may be seen in the note on chap. v. 5, that Ireeneus in the second century has quoted this part, pleasing God, or pleasing to God, and another of the fathers of the church has done the same, and these clearly shew the book of Enoch to be truth.

Verse **23,** This and chap. xvi. 16, are both prophecies of the temple at Jerusalem, for Salem is the name of Jerusalem in Hebrew as may be seen in Buxtorf's Lexicon, and in Psalm Lxxvi. 2, and other places, and it also signifies peace, and the same word and meaning yet remain in the Ethiopic language. And this is proved by the Testament of Levi, who has said, Nevertheless the house which the Lord shall choose, shall be called Jerusalem, as the book of Enoch the righteous containeth. I will also bring here verse 16, of chap. xvi. where it is foretold, that After this the righteous and chosen house of his congregation shall appear henceforth unchangeable in the name of the Lord of spirits. It may be called unchangeable, because the holy Jerusalem, Rev. xxi. 10, will never change, and it is called by the same name. And it may be seen, 2 Chron. vi. 6, that the Almighty had said to David, I have chosen Jerusalem, that my name might be there, and in 1 Kings, viii. 43. in Solomon's prayer at the dedication of the temple, he said, This house which I have builded is called by thy name, that is, the name of the Almighty. This is also a remarkable prophecy of Enoch.

CHAP. XXVII.

Verse 1, This is the description of the luminaries spoken of at chap. xi. 25, which were explained to Enoch by the angel Uriel.

Verse 4, It has been believed, that the first gate answers to the sign Capricorn, which is the most southern point to which the sun reaches, both at rising and setting. The second gate answers to Aquarius; the third to Pisces; the fourth to Aries, when the sun enters into the vernal equinox; (see verse 11) the fifth gate answers to Taurus, (v. 15,) the sixth to Gemini, (verses 17, 18,) the most northern point to which the sun arrives, and turns again to measure back its course to the south. And the same gates which answer to the six signs in the sun's passage from the winter to the summer solstice, also answer to the remaining six signs of the Zodiac in its passage back again viz.: The sixth gate answers to Cancer, (v. 20,) as it did before to Gemini, the fifth Leo, (v. 22,) as before to Taurus, the fourth to Virgo, (v. 24;) as before to Aries, the third to Libra, (v. 27,) as before to Pisces; the second to Scorpio, (v. 39,) as before to Aquarius; the first to Sagittarius, (v. 32,) as before to Capricorn. There is a part of this from verse 4th to verse 11, which is not very plain, but verses 32 to 36 will shew the first gate when the days are at the shortest, and the first gate answers to the sign Capricorn, into which the sun enters, (v. 36,) and it enters into the second gate, (v. 39,) which answers to Aquarius, then into the third, (v. 41,) which answers to Pisces, and at the end of the 31 days, when the sun enters Aries, the day and night are equal as at the beginning of the 11th verse. And every one of Enoch's divisions of the day and night consist of 80 minutes each, for his divisions of day and night being 18, then 18X80=1440, and ours 24X60=1440, which are in minutes the same as the divisions of time used by Enoch. Chapters xxvii. 47, and xxxi. 3,1 corrected a mistake which had formerly been made by some translator in these verses, which was shewn to be a mistake by the next verse.

CHAP. XXVIII.

Verse 15, The meaning seems to be, that when the sun is in Libra, at the autumnal equinox, one of the signs appropriated to the third gate, and when it enters Aries at the venial equinox, one only of the signs appropriated to the fourth gate, the full as well as new moon, rises and sets in the same gates or parts of the heavens as the sun, which cannot be the case at other times of the year.

CHAP. XXIX.

Verse 15, It is likely that these chariots are what is called the milky way.

CHAP. XXX.

Verse 15, This shews that the Most High descends in the south.

Verse 17, This shews that the third part of the north contains paradise, (see note on chap. x. 29.) Perhaps from these words the people who dwelt in the north and south, might think they had a better chance of obtaining eternal life than they who dwell in the east, and west, but our Saviour declared, Mat. viii. 11, That many shall come from east, and west, and shall sit down in the kingdom of heaven.

Verses **19, 20,** The first river has been thought to be the Danube, which flows into the Euxine sea between 46 and 47 degrees of latitude. The two next flowing into the Erythraean sea, have been thought to be the Ganges, and Indus; and the two on the north flowing into the Erythraean sea, the Euphrates, and Tigris; and the latter two the Don, and Volga, one of them pouring into the Euxine sea, the other into the Caspian sea, which the ancients generally believed to have a secret union.

CHAP. XXXI.

Verse **1,** The word Or, in Hebrew signifies light, and yares appears to be derived from heres or cheres, one of the Hebrew names of the sun, so Oryares may signify the sun, or the shining sun, and Tomas appears to be derived from chammah, or shemesh, other two of the Hebrew names of the sun.

Verse **2,** Asonya appears to be derived from the Hebrew shanah, to change or vary, because the moon is always changing and varying. Ebla appears to be derived from the Hebrew word Hebei, or Habel, to vanish away, fade, and disappear, because the moon vanishes away, fades, and disappears. And Benase appears to be derived from Lebanah, one of the Hebrew names of the moon, and Erae appears to be derived from Yareach, another of the Hebrew names of the moon.

CHAP. XXXII.

Verse **3,** Its decrease &c. This appears to be the meaning, that the moon always passes the most northern point of its rising, or the turning point of the sixth gate, at some time during its wane in one hundred and seventy-seven days, or half of the lunar year. The part of the year alluded to is from the longest to the shortest day of the year. This must be the case, because the place of the full moon, from which its wane commences, as being always opposite to the sun, falls short during the time mentioned of the sign Cancer, the turning point of the sixth gate, and the reverse holds good during the other half of the year, while the sun is proceeding from the shortest to the longest day. Of this an account is given at chap. xxxi. 19, 20.

Verses **8 to 15,** These appear to be a prediction of the evils to happen before the flood, which was foretold in the 15th and 25th verses.

CHAP. XXXIII.

Verse **2,** This clearly shews that the book had been written by Enoch.

Verse **11,** Four conductors enter, &c,, after these twelve &c. The names of the four first are in verses 12, 13, and the other names in the chapter are just twelve, but it is not shewn what they are in this place, but. it may be seen in chap. xix. 23, 24, 25, 26, 27, 28, that frost, hail, snow, mist, dew, and rain are all brought forth by angels, and it may be seen by chap. xxvii. l, and xxviii. 11, That Uriel was the holy angel who conducted them all; therefore it is likely that all the other conductors will he angels, I shall here give an explanation of the meanings of the names of the conductors, which names appear to be derived from the Hebrew:

Melkel, a strong ruler.
Helammelek, a powerful ruler.
Melial, he rules the multitude.
Narel, great splendour,
Adnarel, to the light.
Jyasusael, very great joy.
Jyelumiel, strength above.
Melkias, having power.
Barkel, a powerful blessing.
Zelsabel, the great host in shades.
Heloyaleph, the strong ruler of a thousand.
Helammelek, the powerful ruler.
Gedaeyel, the powerful troop.
Keel, powerful.
Heel, fortitude.
Asphael, a strong gatherer together.

CHAP. XXXIV.

Verse **1,** &c., This is a wonderful vision of the destruction of the old world.

CHAP. XXXV.

Verse **1,** Enoch's vision; ver. 2, creation of Adam; ver. 4, and Eve, Cain, and Abel; ver. 5, Cain kills Abel; ver. 7, Cain's children; ver. 8, Eve sought for Abel; ver. 10, Adam came to her; ver. 11, Seth born; ver. 12, and several others; ver. 17, Samiaza descended, the leader of the evil angels, (see chap. ii. 3); ver. 19, The rest of the evil angels descended, (see chap. ii. 7, also Gen. vi. 2, 4); ver. 23, They also began to devour the animals, that was when the giants began to eat the flesh of men, (Enoch, ii. 24); ver. 24, There came from heaven four white men, these were the four great archangels, Michael, Gabriel, Raphael, and Uriel, as it is shewn in Chap. iii. 1; ver. 27, This would be Raphael, who bound Azaziel, who was not the first who descended, chap. ii. 3, but the first or chief leader into wickedness, (chap. iv. 12), see also chap. iii. 5.

Verse **30,** This would be the angel Gabriel, (chap iv. 13) who sent them one against another, and this clearly shews that there had been a battle of the giants.

Verse **31,** This would be the angel Michael, the leader and chief prince, Dan. x. 13, who was commanded to bind them all, chap. iv. 15.

CHAP. XXXVI.

Verse 1, This would be the angel Uriel sent to Noah, (chap. iv. 2, 3, 4,) who made the ark, (Gen. vi. 14,) and with his three sons entered into the ark, (Gen. vii. 13); ver. 2, The flood came; ver. 7, Every living creature perished, except those which were with Noah in the ark, (Gen. vii. 21); ver. 12 Noah and his sons went out of the ark, (Gen. viii. 18); ver. 13, One of Noah's sons was like him, that was Japhet, whose name is derived from the Hebrew yaphah, or Japhah, which signifies beautiful. One of them was red, that was Shem, the meaning of which in Hebrew is name, and it is likely that Noah would be made to understand, that He whose name is great and wonderful, Joshua, or Jesus, the blessed Saviour, would receive the nature of man from the descendants of Shem. And one was black, that was Ham, whose name in Hebrew by many is written Cham, which word in Hebrew signifies warm perhaps Noah might have some foreknowledge of the warm climate, which was to be inhabited by the descendants of Ham, who in Scripture are called Ethiopians, which word is derived from the Greek Aithos, black, and Opsis face, because these people have black faces.

Verse **17,** Abraham, (Gen. xii. 1,) ver. 18, Ishmael, Isaac, (Gen. xxi. 5,) Abraham's children by Keturah, (Gen. xxv. 2,) Esau, and Jacob, ver. 19, Esau's children, (Gen. xxxvi.) ver. 20, The twelve sons of Jacob, ver. 21, Joseph sold to the Ishmaelites, (Gen. xxxvii. 28,) ver. 22, Joseph sold to the Egyptians, (Gen. xxxvii. 36,) ver. 24, Joseph's brethren went to Egypt, (Gen. xlvi. 3,) ver. 27, The Egyptians destroyed their children, (Exod. i. 22,) ver. 28, Moses, (Exod. ii. 15,) verses 29, 30, (see Exod. ii. 23, 24, 25,) ver. 31, (see Exod. iii. 10,) ver. 32, Aaron, (see Exod. iv. 14,) ver. 33, (see Exod. v. 1,) ver. 34, (see Exod. v. 21,) ver. 35, The plagues of Egypt, (see Exod. vii. 20, &c.) ver. 36, The Israelites depart, (see Exod. xii. 37,) ver. 38, They came to the Red Sea, (Exod. xiv. 9.)

CHAP. XXXVII.

Verse **1,** The red sea divided, (see Exod. xiv. 21,) ver 2, He placed &c. (see Exod. xiv. 19, 20,) ver. 3, (see Exod. xiv. 23,) ver. 4, (see Exod. xiv. 25,) ver. 5, (see Exod. xiv. 27,) ver. 6, (Exod. xv. 22,) ver. 7, (Exod. xvi. 13, 14, and xvii. 6,) ver. 8, Moses, ver. 9, (Exod. xix. 3, 10,) ver. 10, 11, (see Exod. xix. 16,) ver. 12, (Exod. xx. 19,) ver. 13, (Exod. xxiv. 12,) ver. 14, (Exod. xxxii. 1,) ver. 15, (Exod. xxxii. 7,) verses 16, 17, (Exod. xxxii. 15, 19,) verses 18, 19, (Exod. xxxii. 22,) ver. 20, 21. (Exod. xxxii. 28,) ver. 22, (see Exod. xxxiii. 7,) ver. 23, Aaron's death, (see Numbers, xx. 28,) ver. 24, Moses' death, (see Deut. xxxiv. 5,) ver. 25, (Deut. xxxiv. 8,) ver. 26, The river Jordan passed, (see Joshua, iii. 16,) ver. 27, The

Judges of Israel, (see Judges, iii. 9, &c.) ver. 29, another sheep. Samuel, (see 1 Sam. vii. 6, 15,) ver. 30, another sheep that was Saul, (1 Sam. x. 21, &c.) ver. 31, (see 1 Sam. xv. 11,) ver. 33, 34, Samuel went to anoint David, (1 Sam. xvi. 13,) ver. 35, (see 1 Sam. xix. 1,) ver. 36, David fled, (see 1 Sam. xx. 42,) ver. 36, The Philistines caused the death of Saul, (see 1 Sam. xxxi. 4,) ver. 37, (see 2 Sam. ii. 4,) ver. 38, (see 1 Kings, ii. 10.)

CHAP. XXXVIII.

Verse 1, That was Solomon, (1 Kings i. 39,) ver. 4. (See 1 Kings ii. 25,) ver. 5, (see 1 Kings vii. 51,) ver. 7, (see 1 Kings viii. 5,) ver. 9, the prophets, ver. 10, Elijah, (see 1 Kings xix. 2,) ver. 11, Elijah taken to heaven, (see 2 Kings ii. 11,) ver. 12, the prophets, ver. 16, The beginning of the captivity, ver. 18, These seventy shepherds would be the great Sanhedrim of the Jews, consisting of seventy or seventy-two persons, who presided over the affairs of all that nation from the time of the captivity, till the destruction of Jerusalem, except some of the time of Hircanus, when the form of government was changed by Gabinius, president of Syria, yet the power of the Sanhedrim remained in another form, and it is shewn in **Chap.** xxxix. 45, that the seventy shepherds were condemned to punishment, and that will clearly shew that the kings of Judah could not be part of these shepherds, for David, Hezekiah, Josiah, and others of the kings of Judah were righteous men, who would not be condemned to punishment; ver. 25, The Babylonian captivity ver. 31, One of the holy angels, (see **Chap.** viii. l, and xxxix. 44,) ver. 35, Zerrubbabel, Jeshua and Nehemiah, (see Ezra. v. 2, and Nehemiah, iii. 1,) ver. 36, The Samaritans; ver. 42, The angel, as at ver. 31.

CHAP. XXXIX.

Verse 1, These shepherds according to the way in which they are here described, appear to be the kings of Judah and Israel. The thirty-five kings of Judah and Israel are these, Of Judah,1» Rehoboam, 2, Abijam, 3, Asa, 4, Jehoshaphat, 5, Jehoram, 6, Ahaziah, 7, Athaliah, 8, Joash, 9, Amaziah, 10, Azariah, 11,

Jotham, 12, Ahaz, 13, Hezekiah, 14, Manasseh, 15, Amon, 16, Josiah, 17, Jehoiakim, 18, Jehoiachin, 19, Zedekiah; Of Israel, 1, Jeroboam, 2, Nadab, 3, Baasha, 4, Elah, 5, Omri, 6, Ahab, 7, Ahaziah, 8, Joram, 9, Jehu, 10, Jehoahaz, 11, Jehoash, 12, Jeroboam II. 13, Menahem, 14, Pekahiah, 15, Pekah, 16, Hoshea. Now the first 19, and these 16, make 35. But in this list Jehoahaz son of Josiah is omitted among the kings of Judah, who reigned only 3 months, and Zachariah who after Jeroboam II. reigned only 6 months, there were thirty-five before, and these two make thirty-seven shepherds, but these two last are not numbered in the times at verse 7th, because neither of them reigned a year, which appears to be a time.

Verse 7, The twenty-three shepherds appear to be the kings of Babylon, Persia, and Macedon, who ruled over the Israelites till the time of Mattathias. The kings of Babylon were four, viz. Nebuchadnezzar, Evilmerodach, Neriglissar, and Belshazzar. The Persian kings were eleven, Darius the Mede, Cyrus, Cambyses, Darius Hystaspis, Xerxes, Artaxerxes Longimanus, Darius Nothus, Artaxerxes Mnemon, Ochus, Arogus, and Darius. The Macedonian kings were eight, Alexander, Ptolemy Soter, Ptolemy Philadelphus, Ptolemy Euergetes, Ptolemy Philopater, Antiochus the great, Seleucus Philopater, and Antiochus Epiphanes. These added together make 23, which with the 35 mentioned in the note at verse 1st, make 58.

Verse **15,** The dabela appears to be Mattathias, and his sons. The dabela lamented (1 Mac. ii. 6.)

Verse **20,** The wars of Judas Maccabeus and his brethren with the heathen.

Verses **21, 22,** The fulfilment of this prophecy is shewn, 2 Mac. x. 29, For when the battle waxed strong, there appeared unto the enemies five comely men upon horses, with bridles of gold, and two of them led the Jews, and took Maccabeus between them, and the angel was one of the 7 at chap. viii. 1, and *Verse* 45.

Verse **24,** They strove to destroy the power of the Jews.

Verse **25,** The Lord of the sheep smote the earth &c. This appears to be the smiting of Antiochus Epiphanes, as described in 2 Maccabees ix. 7, for men are called sons of the earth in this book chap. vii. 2, and other places, and as the name Adam in

Hebrew signifies earth, there might be a difficulty in translating this part correctly out of Hebrew into Ethiopic. And the smiting and fall of Antiochus Epiphanes were also foretold by Ezekiel in **Chap.** xxxix. 3, 4, 5, where he is called Gog. And from these and other places of Scripture it appears to be evident that the smiting of the earth, was the smiting of the wicked ruler of that part of the earth, who was called Antiochus Epiphanes.

Verse **25,** I saw that the Jews or others who had taken the prophecies of the life, death, resurrection, and ascension, of our blessed Saviour out of the book of Enoch, had also transposed several verses of this chapter, and put them into wrong places, by which they could not be understood, but I have corrected them. The verse which was the 25th, is now the 28th, and these which were the 26th, 27th, 28th, are now the 25th, 26th, 27th, and these which were 38, 39, 40, are now 29, 30, 31, and that which was 41, is 40, and these which were 42, 43, 44, 45, 46, 47, 48, 49, are now 32, 33, 34, 35, 36, 37, 38, 39, and these which were 29, 30, 31, 32, 33, 34, 35, 36, 37, are now 41, 42, 43, 44, 45, 46, 47, 48, 49, and the prophecies can now he easily understood, and the places of Scripture pointed out which shew their fulfilment.

Verses **26, 27,** This was when the power of Antiochus Epiphanes and his successors were overthrown. Verse 28, One of the angels whose names are at verse 44.

Verse **28,** These last twelve shepherds would be Mattathias, Judas Maccabeus, Jonathan, Simon, John Hyrcanus, Aristobulus, Alexander Janneus, Alexandra his widow, Aristobulus, Hyrcanus, Antigonus, and Herod, some of these destroyed many Jews, particularly Alexander Janneus, and the Pharisees in the time of Alexandra, and many were destroyed by Herod.

Verse **30,** This appears to have been the rebuilding of the temple by Herod.

Verse **31,** This appears to have been fulfilled, 2 Maccabees iii. 2, or 1 Maccabees xv. 16, &c.

Verse **33,** This appears to have been before the birth of our Saviour, because there was peace at that time.

Verse **35,** A white being was born. This was our blessed Saviour.

Verse **37,** It is proved by the gospel of St. John, chap. i. 1, that this was our Saviour, who is also called the Word of God in Rev, xix. 13. It is certain that a part has been taken out of the book of Enoch in this place, by the Jews or others. This part contained a prophecy of the life, death, resurrection, and ascension of our blessed Saviour by Enoch, of which I shall bring a part from the Testaments of Levi, and Benjamin, who plainly shew that they have read it in the book of Enoch the righteous, for Levi said, And truly my children, I know by the writings of Enoch that in the end ye shall do wickedly, laying your hands most spitefully upon the Lord, and through you your brethren shall be confounded, and be made a scorning stock to all nations. Howbeit, our father Israel is clear from the wickedness of the high priests, who shall lay hands upon the Saviour of the world. And in another place he said, Furthermore, I know by the book of Enoch, that ye shall go astray by the space of threescore and ten weeks, and defile the priesthood, stain the sacrifices, destroy the law, despise the sayings of the prophets, frowardly persecute righteous people, hate the godly, abhor the sayings of sooth-fast men, and call him heretic that goeth about to renew the law by the power of the Highest, and in the end you shall kill him out of hand as you think, not knowing that he shall rise again, and so ye shall receive his innocent blood willfully upon your own heads. For his sake your holy places shall be left desolate, which you shall have defiled even by utter forswearing, and your dwelling shall not be clean, but you shall be accursed among the heathen, and despair shall vex you, till he visit you again and mercifully receive you through faith and water. But there is more of this prophecy, for Levi declared, That after the Lord hath sent vengeance upon them in the priesthood, then God will raise up a new priest (1) unto whom all the Lord's words shall be opened, and there shall be peace (2) over all the earth, and his star (3) shall arise in heaven, and the angels (4) of glory who are in the presence of the Lord shall rejoice in him. The heavens (5) shall be opened, and out of the temple of glory sanctification shall come upon him with the voice of the Father, and he shall execute true judgment on earth many days, and as a king (6) he shall send forth the light of knowledge in the open sunshine (7) of the day, and he shall be magnified (8) over all the world, and be received and shine (9) as the sun upon the earth, and drive (10) away all darkness. In his days the heavens shall rejoice, the earth shall be glad, the clouds shall be joyful, the knowledge (11) of the Lord shall be poured out upon the earth as the waters of the sea, and the glory (12) of the Highest shall be spread out upon him, whereof he shall give abundantly and mightily to his children in truth for evermore, and there shall none succeed him from generation to generation world without end. In his priesthood all sin (13) shall come to an end, and he shall open (14) the gates of paradise, and stay the threatening sword against Adam, and feed the lambs (15) with the fruit of life, and the spirit of holiness shall be in them. He shall bind up Belial, (16) and give his own children power (17) to tread down hurtful spirits, and the Lord shall rejoice in his children, and accept them as his beloved for evermore. This last part of the prophecy of Enoch preserved by Levi, I have transposed in some places, to make its fulfilment more intelligible. The following is in the Testament of Benjamin, which I have translated from the Greek, more correctly than it has formerly been translated, But I know all your deeds, and the good which shall be in you from the words of Enoch the righteous. For ye shall commit fornication like the fornication of Sodom, and ye shall be lost for a while, and ye shall renew your wantonness with women, and the kingdom of the Lord shall not be in you, because he will quickly take it away. But the temple of the Lord shall be in a part of you, and in you there shall be glory, for he shall receive it, and there he shall bring the twelve tribes, and all nations, when the Highest shall send his salvation (18) in the visitation of his only begotten. And he shall be brought into the chief place (19) of judgment, and there the Lord shall be insulted, (20) and shall be raised up on a cross (21) and the vail (22) of the temple shall be rent, and he shall arise (23) out of the grave, and shall ascend (24) from the earth into heaven, and the Spirit (25) of God shall go forth upon the nations poured out as fire. And that alone shall be known (26) to all the humble upon earth, and that alone shall be glorious in heaven. Now this prophecy of our blessed Saviour by Enoch was the principal of the scriptures which he said must be fulfilled, Mat. xxvi. 59, and its fulfilment may be seen in the New Testament. I shall point out a few places, first from the part preserved by Levi, (1) Priest, see Heb. iv. 14, (2) Peace, &c., see the Roman history of that time, (3) Star, &c., see Mat. ii. 2, (4) Angels, &c , see Luke ii. 13, 14, (5) Heavens, &c., see Mat. iii. 16, 17, (6) King, &c., see Luke xix. 38, (7) Open sunshine, see John zviii. 20, (8) Magnified, Mat. xxi. 15, John xii 13, (9) shine, see John viii. 12, (10) drive, see Mat. iv. 16, (11) Knowledge, see Mat. chap. v. and vi. and vii. and John chap. xv. and xvi. and xvii. (12) glory &c., John i. 14, (13) Sin, &c., see 1 John ii. 2, (14) Gates, &c., see John x. 7, (15) Lambs, &c., see John x. 9,10, (16) Belial, see Mat. xii. 28, 29, (17) Power, &c., see Luke x. 17. Now the following are in that part of the prophecy which is preserved by Benjamin, (18) Salvation, &c., see John iii. 16, (19) Chief place, &c., see John xviii. 28, (20) Insulted, see John xix 3, (21) Cross, see John xix. 17,18,19, (22) Vail, &c., see Mat. xxvii. 51, (23) Arise, &c., see Mat. xxviii. 6, (24) Ascend, &c., see Acts i. 9, (25) Spirit of God, &c., see Acts ii. 3,4, (26) Known &c., see Acts ii. 6.

Verse **40,** Before had caused me to ascend, see chapter xxxv. 25,

Verse **44,** The seven white ones were the angels, chap. viii. 1. Michael, Gabriel, Raphael, Phanuel, Sarakiel, and Uriel, and also Raguel. The first of the stars appears to be Azaziel, because he was the first in wickedness, see chap. iv. 12, and the note on chap. xxxv. 27; and the first star which fell down first, was Samiaza, see chap. ii. 3.

Verse **45,** This is one of the seven angels mentioned in verse 44, he appears to be the same, who is mentioned in Ezekiel ix. 3, and Daniel xii. 6, and one of the seven angels mentioned in Rev. v. 6. and Zachariah iv. 10, and the seventy shepherds were the Jewish Sanhedrim, see note on chapter xxxviii. 18.

Verse **48,** This deep would be the valley of the son of Hinnom in Hebrew Gehinnom, from which the Greek word geene, (hell) is derived, according to Buxtorf's Lexicon.

CHAP. XL.

Verse 6, An end of all unrighteousness appears to be a prediction of the flood of Noah.

CHAP. XLI.

Verse 7, This prophecy of the ten weeks is a very remarkable prophecy
In the first week Enoch was born;

In the second there was great wickedness;

In the third, the deluge was upon the earth, and Abraham was called;

In the fourth week, the law was given on mount Sinai, and the tabernacle made;

In the fifth, Solomon's temple was built;

In the sixth week, which ended 196 years after Christ, the Jews were darkened, their hearts were forgetful of wisdom, and our blessed Saviour ascended into heaven, and in its accomplishment, the temple was burnt with fire, and the Jews dispersed.

In the seventh week, which ended 896 years after Christ, there were six persecutions, there were ten horns or kingdoms founded out of the Romish empire, and subject to the Pope. The Bishop of Rome was constituted universal head of the church. Mahomet established his religion. And the Popes became civil Lords in Italy, whence they gradually claimed dominion over all the earth. In these there were abundance of perverse deeds, but Constantine was converted, and heathenism abolished.

In the eighth week, which ended 1596 years after Christ, many of the states of Europe threw off the dominion of the Pope, and the Roman Catholics were delivered into the hands of the righteous Protestants; and the house of the great King was built up for ever by doing and teaching righteousness, see 1 Peter ii. 5, Ephes, ii. 20,21, Epistle of Barnabas xiii 16, 17, 19, 20, 21, 22,24.

The ninth week will end 2296 years after Christ, and as it is the time in which we are now living, it may be seen by the great number of societies for the propagation of the gospel, in many different parts of the earth, that the judgment of righteousness is in a fair way of being revealed to the whole world, and it is likely that it will be more fully revealed about the year of our Lord 2000, which is believed to be about the beginning of the millennium.

Enoch's weeks according to the Chronology in a large bible:

CREATION,	4	Years before Christ.	
	004		
	7		
	00		
	———		
End of 1st week.	3		
	304		
	7		
	00		
End of 2nd week.	2	Wickedness.	
	604	Deluge.	B.C.
	7	Abraham called.	2349
	00		1921

End of 3rd week.	1		
	904	The law given on mount Sinai and	
	7	the Tabernacle made.	1491
	00		
End of 4th week.	1		
	204	Solomon's Temple finished.	1004
	7		
	00		
End of 5th week.	5		
	04	Our blessed Saviour ascen.	33
	7	The Temple destroyed and the	
	00	Jews dispersed.	70
End of 6th week }	1		
After Christ. }	96	Six persecutions.	
	7		
	00		
End of 7th week.	8	Opposers of the Popes.	
	96	Wickliff.	1369
	7	Luther.	1517
	00	Henry VIII	1533
		Edward VI	1547
		Spanish Armada defeated.	1588
End of 8th week.	1		
	596		
	7		
	00		
End of 9th week.	2	Millennium begins.	1996
	296	Everlasting judgment }	2896
	7	from	2996
	00	Upon the watchers } to	
End of 10th week.	2		
	296		
	4		
	004		
700 X 10	7		
	000		
	7		
	000		

This I think can need no explanation, except at the end of the fifth week, when the number was 504; I subtracted that from 700 years, the time of the sixth week, and there remained 196 years after Christ, and it may be seen in the large bibles, that four of the first years after the time of the birth of our Saviour are left out.

Enoch's weeks from the Creation, each week being 700 years:

End of 1st week.	70		
	0	Wickedness.	
	70		
	0		
End of 2nd week.	14	Deluge, in the year of the world.	1655
	00	Abraham called.	2083
	70		
	0		
End of 3rd week.	21		
	00	The law given upon mount Sinai,	
	70	and the Tabernacle made.	2513
	0		
End of 4th week.	28		
	00	Solomon's Temple finished.	3000
	70		
	0		
End of 5th week.	35		
	00	Our blessed Saviour ascen.	4037
	70	The Temple destroyed and the	
	0	Jews dispersed.	4074
End of 6th week	42		
	00	Six persecutions.	
	70		
	0		
End of 7th week.	49	Opposers of the Popes.	
	00	Wickliff.	5373
	70	Luther.	5521
	0	Henry VIII	5537
		Edward VI	5551
		Spanish Armada defeated.	5592
End of 8th week.	56		
	00	Millennium begins.	6000
	70		

0

End of 9th week.	63	Everlasting judgment	}	6900
	00	from		
	70	Upon the watchers	} to	7000
	0			
End of 10th week.	70			
	00			

It may be seen by the Chronology in the large Bibles, that the deluge was 2349 years before Christ, and by subtracting this from 4004 the time that the Creation of the world was before Christ, it will shew that the flood was 1655 years after the creation of the world. And what happened after the birth of our Saviour should have 4004 years added to the years after Christ, according to the chronology in the large bibles, to make it agree with this. And it may be seen in the large bibles, that four of the first years after the time of the birth of our Saviour are left out.

In Enoch's ninth week there will be 300 years of the time called the millennium, and Enoch in verses 17, 18, has shewn that the beginning of it will be in that week, by prophesying that the judgment of righteousness shall be revealed to the whole world, and he has also foretold that it will be about 7000 years from the creation of the world, to the time when the judgment will be finished, and this prophecy of Enoch agrees with the Jewish tradition attributed to Elijah, by which it is foretold that the world will continue 6000 years, these thousands being according to the number of the days in which all things were created, and a sabbath of a thousand years of great peace and plenty, at the coming of the Messiah. The same is partly described by Moses, Psalm xc. 4, For a thousand years are in the sight of the Almighty as yesterday. And it is more fully described by St. Peter 2 Peter iii. 8, But beloved, be not ignorant of this one thing, that one day is with the Lord as a thousand years, and a thousand years as one day; and then he gives a description of the general judgment. And the millennium is described by St. John in Rev. xx. 4, I saw thrones, and they sat on them, and judgment was given to them, and he shews that the souls of the righteous lived and reigned with Christ a thousand years. But the whole is described by St. Barnabas in his Epistle, chap. xiii. 3, 4, 5, 6, 9, That in six thousand years the Lord God will bring all things to an end, for with him one day is a thousand years, that when his Son shall come, and abolish the season of the wicked one, and judge the ungodly, and change the sun, moon, and stars, then shall he gloriously rest upon the seventh day. And this prophecy of Enoch would be well known in the time of Moses therefore he has only mentioned a part in his Psalm, and it has been shewn by Archbishop Wake in a note on the 13th chapter of the Epistle of Barnabas, that this opinion was very common in the time of the apostles, therefore St. Peter has only described a part of it. But both Moses and St. Peter have given descriptions which clearly shew that they knew the truth of this prophecy.

Verse **21,** This shews that in the new heaven sin shall not be mentioned for ever and ever, and it is proved by Rev. xxi. 27, where it is foretold of the holy Jerusalem, There shall in no wise "enter into it any thing that defileth, or worketh abomination, or maketh a lie. This is another proof of the truth of the prophecies of Enoch.

CHAP. XLII.

Verse **1,** Here Enoch had given his children most excellent instruction.

Verse **14,** Here it is shewn that the wicked shall be under the dominion of the righteous.

Verse **22,** The deepest spring. Perhaps this may mean the strongest liquor.

Verse **23,** Water at pleasure may also mean liquor. The fountain of life is the Almighty, Jer. ii. 13.

CHAP. XLIII.

Verse 4, When the day, &c. This is proved, Mat x. 26, by our blessed Saviour, For there is nothing covered, which shall not be revealed, and again in Mat. xii. 26, Every idle word that men shall speak, they shall give account thereof in the day of judgment. This is another proof of the truth of the prophecies of Enoch.

Verse 12, Mountain and hill appear to denote people eminent for righteousness, and it is clear that none eminent for righteousness will be a servant or a slave to the vices of a wicked woman.

CHAP. XLIV.

Verses 7, 8, These verses were quoted by Tertullian, who knew the truth of the book of Enoch.

CHAP. XLV.

Verse 2, This is a description of the general judgment.

Verses 8, 9, It is here shewn that the sun, moon, and stars, the clouds, snow, dew, and rain, will all bear witness against the wicked at the great day of judgment. Now it is evident from this and **Chap.** xliii. 4, 15, and the proofs brought forward there, that all the places where wickedness has been committed, will be made to appear again by the Almighty at the great day of judgment, and that all kinds of wickedness, however secretly they may have been committed, will all be so clearly proved, that there will not be the least chance of keeping any thing secret at that awful day. Now what is here shewn ought to be well considered by people when on earth, because there is no repentance after the earthly body is dead, and they who will be driven away at the day of judgment, will be driven away to everlasting punishment.

CHAP. XLVI.

Verses **9, 10,** This clearly shews the great joy and happiness prepared in heaven for the souls of the righteous.

Verse **12,** This shews the dreadful punishment of the wicked.

CHAP. XLVII.

Verse **2,** This shews that the righteous shall shine like the lights of heaven, and it is proved by Dan. xii. 2, and by Mat. xiii. 43, when our Saviour said, Then shall the righteous shine forth as the sun in the kingdom of their Father. This also proves the truth of the book of Enoch.

Verse **13,** This shews that the Almighty and his Son will be for ever united with the righteous in the ways of righteousness, and it is proved 1 John i. 3, And truly our fellowship is with the Father, and with his Son Jesus Christ. This also proves the truth of the book of Enoch.

CHAP. XLVIII.

Verse **2,** This description of the birth of Noah is very remarkable, yet there are several things more wonderful than it described in Scripture, the dividing of the red sea, the bringing of water from a rock, and many others, but because Noah was to preserve the race of mankind, these wonderful things at has birth might be caused by the Almighty, that the people in time to come might see his power in preserving the righteous. And it appears to be shewn from verses 13 to 19, that many remarkable things relating to Noah, had been known by Enoch before that time.

Verse **26,** This shews that the Almighty will place every one of the righteous on a throne of glory, and it is proved by Rev. i. 6, and by Rev. iii. 21, when our Saviour said to St. John, To him that overcometh will I grant to sit with me in my throne. This prophecy is not in the books of the Old Testament, and it is another proof of the truth of the prophecies of Enoch.

INDEX.

Balance, to weigh the works of men, xiii. 10, and xx. 11.
Beginning of wisdom, not to be hindered, xii. 2.
Behemoth, in Hebrew signifies wild beasts, &c., xix. 8.
Blessing of Enoch, i. 1,
Bow and sword of fire, viii. 10.

Cherubim, Seraphim, and Ophanin shall bless, &c., xx. 13, and xxvi 13.
Clouds, snow, dew, and rain, witnesses against sinners, xlv. 9.
Conductors of the stars, names of, xxxiii 10,12,13, &c.
Countenance of the Son of man full of grace, xiv. 6.
Creator of days seen by Enoch, xiv. 6, and xxvi. 16,20.
Creator of days on the throne of his glory, xiv. 14, and xix. 1.

Decree of the Almighty, its power, xxv. 19, 21.
Deeds evil, all revealed in heaven, xliii. 4,15.
Deluge foretold, xlviii. 14.
Dispersion of the Jews foretold, xli. 14.
Divisions three between the spirits of the dead, x. 9.

Earth to be renewed, xiv. 5.
Elect One, xiii. 5, and xiv 4, and xv. 5, 13, 24, and xvi. 5, 10 and xx. 13, & xxi. 1.
Elect One, on a throne of glory, xiv. 3, and xv. 22, and xvii. 5 and xx. 10.
Elect shall be preserved, and happy, i. 7, 23.
Elect and holy sung before the Lord of spirits, xii. 16.
Enoch spoke with the holy and mighty One, i. 3.
Enoch praised God, v. 3, and x. 15, 31, and xi. 7, 36, and xii. 19, 21, and xxxii. 19.
Enoch concealed, v. 1.
Enoch sent to the fallen angels, v. 5.
Enoch had power to reprove the watchers, vi. 2.
Enoch's visions, vi. 9, and xii. 1, and xxxiv. 1. and xxxv. 1 & xii. 6.
Enoch wished to remain in heaven, xii. 17.
Enoch, spirit of, concealed in heaven, xxvi. 10.
Enoch cried with the spirit of power, praising, xxvi. 18.
Enoch pleased God, xxvi. 19.

Michael praised the Almighty, xiii. 4.
Michael and others to be strengthened, xvi. 23.
Millennium, appears to be foretold, xli. 17, 18.
Monsters, to destroy the wicked at the flood, xix. 7, 8.
Moon's path to the righteous light, to sinners darkness, xiii. 5.
Moon, law of, xxviii. 1.
Moon, progress of explained by Uriel, xxviii. 11.
Moon, names of, xxxi. 2.
Most High spoke, and gave commands to the angels, iv. 1.
Mountains, beautiful, x. 21.
Mountains of metal, xvi. 2, 5, and xxiii, 19.
Mouths of the holy full of blessings, xii. 16.

Names of the evil angels, ii. 9, and xxv. 2.
Names of others who seduced them, xxv. 4.
Name of the Lord of spirits shall be praised, xx, 14.
Name of the Son of man exalted, xxvi. 1.
North, life planted in the, x. 29.
None can perish, xx. 7.
Nothing spoken in vain, xxi. 6, and xxiii. 26.

Ophanin, xx. 13, and xxvi. 13.

Paradise presided over by Gabriel, viii. 7.
Paradise, xxx. 17.
Parable first, xii. 4.
Parable second, xiv. I.
Parable third, xviii. 1.
Phanuel drove out the evil angels, xiii. 7.
Pillar of the earth shaken, xvii. 16.
Place of punishment, vi. 12, and xlviii. 22.
Place of happiness, vi. 14.
Place of the elect, xii. 14.
Places delightful for the souls of the dead, x. 1, 3.
Places for the elect & the righteous in the north, xx. 3, and xxvi.
    3.
Power to reprove the watchers given to Enoch, vi. 2.
Prayer of the righteous for judgment, xiv. 13.

Rivers of fire, xxiii. 22.

Sun filled with flaming fire, xxvii. 6.
Sun, names of the, xxxi. 1.
Sun, moon, and other stars witnesses against the wicked, xiv. 8

SAMUEL JEFFERSON, PRINTER, SCOTCH-STREET, CARLISLE.

Appendix to the 21ˢᵗ Century Edition

Readers of the Baty translation of the Book of Enoch already familiar with Enoch's book will notice the very different way in which the translation has been broken into chapters and verses. Actually, the first two translations of the Book of Enoch into the English language, R L Laurence and John Baty, both used systems of chapter and verse numbering which would be later discarded when a more rational system was introduced by R H Charles in 1883. For those seeking a deeper understanding of the Book of Enoch, acquiring a copy of the R H Charles translation will be an indispensable tool.

To facilitate the ability to cross-reference the Baty translation to Charles, the following table is being introduced here.

BATY	CHARLES	BATY	CHARLES	BATY	CHARLES
1:1	1:1	2:24	7:3	4:15	10:12
1:2	1:2	2:24	7:4	4:16	10:13
1:3	1:3	2:24	7:5	4:17	10:14
1:4	1:4	2:24	7:6	4:18	10:15
1:5	1:5	2:13	8:1	4:19	10:16
1:6	1:6	2:14	8:2	4:23	10:17
1:6	1:7	2:15	8:3	4:23	10:18
1:8	1:8	2:24	8:4	4:24	10:19
1:9	1:9	3:1	9:1	4:25	10:20
1:10	2:1	3:2	9:2	4:26	10:21
1:11	2:2	3:3	9:3	4:27	10:22
1:12	2:3	3:3	9:4	4:28	11:1
1:13	3:1	3:4	9:5	4:29	11:2
1:14	4:1	3:5	9:6	5:1	12:1
1:15	5:1	3:6	9:7	5:2	12:2
1:16	5:2	3:7	9:8	5:3	12:3
1:17	5:3	3:8	9:9	5:5	12:4
1:18	5:4	3:10	9:10	5:7	12:5
1:20	5:5	3:13	9:11	5:7	12:6
1:21	5:6	4:1	10:1	5:8	13:1
1:21	5:7	4:3	10:2	5:9	13:2
1:25	5:8	4:5	10:3	5:11	13:3
1:26	5:9	4:6	10:4	5:13	13:4
2:1	6:1	4:7	10:5	5:13	13:5
2:2	6:2	4:9	10:6	5:14	13:6
2:3	6:3	4:10	10:7	5:15	13:7
2:5	6:4	4:12	10:8	5:16	13:8
2:7	6:5	4:13	10:9	5:16	13:9
2:8	6:6	4:14	10:10	5:17	13:10
2:9	6:7	4:15	10:11	6:1	14:1
2:9	6:8				
2:10	7:2				
2:11	7:2				
2:12	7:2				

BATY	CHARLES	BATY	CHARLES	BATY	CHARLES
6:1	14:2	9:6	18:4	10:14	22:13
6:2	14:3	9:7	18:5	10:15	22:14
6:3	14:4	9:8	18:6	10:16	23:1
6:4	14:5	9:10	18:7	10:17	23:2
6:5	14:6	9:10	18:8	10:18	23:3
6:6	14:7	9:10	18:9	10:19	23:4
6:8	14:8	9:11	18:10	10:21	24:1
6:10	14:9	9:12	18:11	10:22	24:2
6:11	14:10	9:13	18:12	10:22	24:3
6:12	14:11	9:14	18:13	10:23	24:4
6:12	14:12	9:15	18:14	10:24	24:5
6:12	14:13	9:16	18:15	10:24	24:6
6:13	14:14	9:16	18:16	10:25	25:1
6:14	14:15	9:17	19:1	10:27	25:2
6:15	14:16	9:18	19:2	10:28	25:3
6:16	14:17	9:19	19:3	10:29	25:4
6:17	14:18	8:1	20:1	10:29	25:5
6:19	14:19	8:2	20:2	10:30	25:6
6:21	14:20	8:3	20:3	10:31	25:7
6:23	14:21	8:4	20:4	11:1	26:1
6:24	14:22	8:5	20:5	11:1	26:2
6:24	14:23	8:6	20:6	11:2	26:3
6:24	14:24	8:7	20:7	11:3	26:4
6:25	14:25	8:7	20:8	11:3	26:5
7:1	15:1	9:20	21:1	11:3	26:6
7:1	15:2	9:21	21:2	11:4	27:1
7:2	15:3	9:22	21:3	11:5	27:2
7:3	15:4	9:22	21:4	11:6	27:3
7:5	15:5	9:22	21:5	11:7	27:4
7:6	15:6	9:22	21:6	11:7	27:5
7:7	15:7	9:23	21:7	11:8	28:1
7:8	15:8	9:24	21:8	11:9	28:2
7:8	15:9	9:25	21:9	11:10	28:3
7:8	15:10	9:25	21:10	11:11	29:1
7:9	15:11	10:1	22:1	11:12	29:2
7:10	15:12	10:2	22:2	11:13	30:1
7:11	16:1	10:3	22:3	11:15	30:2
7:12	16:2	10:4	22:4	11:16	30:3
7:13	16:3	10:5	22:5	11:17	31:1
7:15	16:4	10:6	22:6	11:18	31:2
7:16	16:4	10:7	22:7	11:18	31:3
8:8	17:1	10:9	22:8	11:19	32:1
8:9	17:2	10:9	22:9	11:20	32:2
8:10	17:3	10:11	22:10	11:21	32:3
8:11	17:4	10:12	22:11	11:22	32:4
8:11	17:5	10:13	22:12	11:22	32:5
8:12	17:6				
8:12	17:7				
8:13	17:8				
9:1	18:1				
9:2	18:2				
9:4	18:3				

BATY	CHARLES	BATY	CHARLES	BATY	CHARLES
11:23	32:6	13:12	41:5	15:17	50:2
11:24	33:1	13:12	41:6	15:18	50:3
11:25	33:2	13:14	41:7	15:18	50:4
11:25	33:3	13:15	41:8	15:19	50:5
11:26	33:4	13:16	41:9	15:20	51:1
11:28	34:1	13:17	42:1	15:21	51:2
11:30	34:2	13:18	42:2	15:22	51:3
11:31	34:3	13:18	42:3	15:23	51:4
11:32	35:1	13:19	43:1	15:24	51:5
11:34	36:1	13:19	43:2	16:1	52:1
11:35	36:2	13:20	43:3	16:2	52:2
11:35	36:3	13:20	43:4	16:3	52:3
11:36	36:4	13:20	44:1	16:4	52:4
12:1	37:1	14:1	45:1	16:5	52:5
12:1	37:2	14:2	45:2	16:5	52:6
12:2	37:3	14:3	45:3	16:6	52:7
12:2	37:4	14:4	45:4	16:8	52:8
12:3	37:5	14:5	45:5	16:10	52:9
12:4	38:1	14:5	45:6	16:11	53:1
12:5	38:2	14:6	46:1	16:12	53:2
12:6	38:3	14:6	46:2	16:13	53:3
12:7	38:4	14:7	46:3	16:14	53:4
12:8	38:5	14:8	46:4	16:15	53:5
12:9	38:6	14:9	46:5	16:16	53:6
12:10	39:1	14:9	46:6	16:17	53:7
12:11	39:2	14:10	46:7	16:18	54:1
12:12	39:3	14:11	46:8	16:19	54:2
12:13	39:4	14:12	47:1	16:20	54:3
12:13	39:5	14:13	47:2	16:21	54:4
12:14	39:6	14:14	47:3	16:22	54:5
12:16	39:7	14:15	47:4	16:23	54:6
12:17	39:8	15:1	48:1	16:24	54:7
12:18	39:9	15:2	48:2	16:25	54:8
12:19	39:10	15:3	48:3	16:27	54:9
12:19	39:11	15:4	48:4	16:28	54:10
12:20	39:12	15:4	48:5	17:1	55:1
12:21	39:13	15:5	48:6	17:2	55:2
12:21	39:14	15:6	48:7	17:4	55:3
13:1	40:1	15:7	48:8	17:5	55:4
13:2	40:2	15:8	48:9	17:6	56:1
13:3	40:3	15:10	48:10	17:6	56:2
13:4	40:4	15:12	49:1	17:7	56:3
13:5	40:5	15:13	49:2	17:8	56:4
13:6	40:6	15:14	49:3	17:9	56:5
13:7	40:7	15:15	49:4	17:10	56:6
13:8	40:8	15:16	50:1	17:11	56:7
13:9	40:9				
13:9	40:10				
13:10	41:1				
13:10	41:2				
13:11	41:3				
13:12	41:4				

BATY	CHARLES	BATY	CHARLES	BATY	CHARLES
17:12	56:8	21:2	62:2	23:18	67:3
17:13	57:1	21:5	62:3	23:19	67:4
17:15	57:2	21:7	62:4	23:20	67:5
17:17	57:3	21:8	62:5	23:21	67:6
18:1	58:1	21:10	62:6	23:22	67:7
18:2	58:2	21:10	62:7	23:23	67:8
18:3	58:3	21:11	62:8	23:25	67:9
18:4	58:4	21:12	62:9	23:27	67:10
18:5	58:5	21:12	62:10	23:28	67:11
18:5	58:6	21:12	62:11	23:29	67:12
18:6	59:1	21:15	62:12	23:30	67:13
18:8	59:2	21:15	62:13	23:31	68:1
18:10	59:3	21:16	62:14	24:1	68:2
19:1	60:1	21:18	62:15	24:2	68:3
19:1	60:2	21:18	62:16	24:3	68:4
19:1	60:3	22:1	63:1	24:4	68:5
19:2	60:4	22:2	63:2	25:1	69:1
19:3	60:5	22:3	63:3	25:2	69:2
19:5	60:6	22:6	63:4	25:3	69:3
19:7	60:7	22:7	63:5	25:4	69:4
19:8	60:8	22:8	63:6	25:5	69:5
19:10	60:9	22:9	63:7	25:6	69:6
19:11	60:10	22:10	63:8	25:8	69:7
18:11	60:11	22:11	63:9	25:9	69:8
18:14	60:12	22:13	63:10	25:11	69:9
18:16	60:13	22:15	63:11	25:13	69:10
18:17	60:14	22:16	63:12	25:14	69:11
18:18	60:15	22:17	64:1	25:17	69:12
18:19	60:16	22:17	64:2	25:19	69:13
18:19	60:17	23:1	65:1	25:20	69:14
18:19	60:18	23:2	65:2	25:21	69:15
18:20	60:19	23:3	65:3	25:23	69:16
18:22	60:20	23:4	65:4	25:25	69:17
18:23	60:21	23:5	65:5	25:26	69:18
18:24	60:22	23:6	65:6	25:27	69:19
18:25	60:23	23:7	65:7	25:28	69:20
19:12	60:24	23:8	65:8	25:29	69:21
19:14	60:25	23:9	65:9	25:31	69:22
20:1	61:1	23:9	65:10	25:32	69:23
20:2	61:2	23:10	65:11	25:34	69:24
20:3	61:3	23:11	65:12	25:36	69:25
20:4	61:4	23:12	66:1	25:37	69:26
20:6	61:5	23:14	66:2	25:39	69:27
20:8	61:6	23:15	66:3	25:40	69:28
20:9	61:7	23:16	67:1	25:41	69:29
20:10	61:8	23:17	67:2	26:1	70:1
20:11	61:9				
20:13	61:10				
20:14	61:11				
20:15	61:12				
20:16	61:13				
21:1	62:1				

BATY	CHARLES	BATY	CHARLES	BATY	CHARLES
26:2	70:2	27:43	72:33	30:7	76:8
26:3	70:3	27:44	72:34	30:8	76:9
26:4	70:4	27:45	72:35	30:9	76:10
26:5	71:1	27:46	72:36	30:9	76:11
26:6	71:2	27:47	72:37	30:9	76:12
26:8	71:3	28:1	73:1	30:9	76:13
26:9	71:4	28:2	73:2	30:9	76:13
26:10	71:5	28:3	73:3	30:10	76:13
26:12	71:6	28:4	73:4	30:11	76:13
26:13	71:7	28:6	73:5	30:12	76:14
26:14	71:8	28:6	73:6	30:14	77:1
26:15	71:9	28:7	73:7	30:16	77:2
26:16	71:10	28:9	73:8	30:17	77:3
26:17	71:11	28:11	74:1	30:18	77:4
26:19	71:12	28:12	74:2	30:19	77:5
26:20	71:13	28:14	74:3	30:20	77:6
26:21	71:14	28:15	74:4	30:20	77:7
26:23	71:15	28:15	74:5	30:21	77:8
26:25	71:16	28:16	74:6	31:1	78:1
26:27	71:17	28:17	74:7	31:2	78:2
27:1	72:1	28:19	74:8	31:3	78:3
27:2	72:2	28:20	74:9	31:4	78:4
27:3	72:3	28:21	74:10	31:4	78:5
27:6	72:4	28:22	74:11	31:5	78:6
27:7	72:5	28:23	74:12	31:7	78:7
27:9	72:6	28:23	74:13	31:9	78:8
27:11	72:7	28:24	74:14	31:10	78:9
27:12	72:8	28:24	74:15	31:12	78:10
27:13	72:9	28:25	74:16	31:13	78:11
27:14	72:10	28:26	74:17	31:14	78:12
27:15	72:11	29:1	75:1	31:15	78:13
27:16	72:12	29:3	75:2	31:16	78:14
27:17	72:13	29:4	75:3	31:19	78:15
27:18	72:14	29:10	75:4	31:20	78:16
27:20	72:15	29:11	75:5	31:21	78:17
27:21	72:16	29:12	75:6	32:1	79:1
27:22	72:17	29:13	75:7	32:2	79:2
27:23	72:18	29:15	75:8	32:2	79:3
27:24	72:19	29:15	75:9	32:3	79:4
27:25	72:20	30:1	76:1	32:4	79:5
27:26	72:21	30:2	76:2	32:5	79:6
27:27	72:22	30:2	76:3	32:6	80:1
27:28	72:23	30:3	76:4	32:8	80:2
27:30	72:24	30:4	76:5	32:10	80:3
27:31	72:25	30:5	76:6	32:11	80:4
27:33	72:26	30:6	76:7	32:12	80:5
27:35	72:27				
27:37	72:28				
27:39	72:29				
27:40	72:30				
27:41	72:31				
27:42	72:32				

BATY	CHARLES	BATY	CHARLES	BATY	CHARLES
32:13	80:7	35:5	85:4	37:15	89:33
32:15	80:8	35:6	85:5	37:19	89:34
32:16	81:1	35:8	85:6	37:20	89:35
32:17	81:2	35:10	85:7	37:22	89:36
32:19	81:3	35:11	85:8	37:23	89:37
32:21	81:4	35:13	85:9	37:24	89:38
32:22	81:5	35:15	85:10	37:27	89:39
32:24	81:6	35:16	86:1	37:28	89:40
32:24	81:7	35:19	86:2	37:29	89:41
32:25	81:8	35:20	86:3	37:30	89:42
32:26	81:9	35:21	86:4	37:30	89:43
32:27	81:10	35:22	86:5	37:31	89:44
33:1	82:1	35:23	86:6	37:33	89:45
33:3	82:2	35:24	87:1	37:34	89:46
33:3	82:3	35:24	87:2	37:35	89:47
33:4	82:4	35:25	87:3	38:1	89:48
33:6	82:5	35:26	87:4	38:4	89:49
33:6	82:6	35:27	88:1	38:5	89:50
33:8	82:7	35:28	88:2	38:8	89:51
33:8	82:8	35:30	88:3	38:11	89:52
33:9	82:9	36:1	89:1	38:12	89:53
33:10	82:10	36:2	89:2	38:13	89:54
33:11	82:11	36:3	89:3	38:15	89:55
33:12	82:12	36:5	89:4	38:16	89:56
33:13	82:13	36:7	89:5	38:17	89:57
33:14	82:14	36:8	89:6	38:18	89:58
33:16	82:15	36:9	89:7	38:19	89:59
33:18	82:16	36:11	89:8	38:20	89:60
33:19	82:17	36:12	89:9	38:21	89:61
33:20	82:18	36:14	89:10	38:22	89:62
33:21	82:19	36:18	89:11	38:23	89:63
33:23	82:20	36:19	89:12	38:24	89:64
34:1	83:1	36:21	89:13	38:25	89:65
34:2	83:2	36:25	89:14	38:25	89:66
34:3	83:3	36:26	89:15	38:26	89:67
34:5	83:4	36:28	89:16	38:28	89:68
34:7	83:5	36:31	89:17	38:29	89:69
34:7	83:6	36:32	89:18	38:32	89:70
34:8	83:7	36:34	89:19	38:33	89:71
34:10	83:8	36:35	89:20	38:36	89:72
34:10	83:9	36:36	89:21	38:37	89:73
34:11	83:10	36:37	89:22	38:40	89:74
34:12	83:11	36:38	89:23	38:41	89:75
34:14	84:1	37:1	89:24	38:42	89:76
34:15	84:2	37:3	89:25	38:42	89:77
34:16	84:3	37:4	89:26	39:1	90:1
34:17	84:4	37:5	89:27	39:2	90:2
34:18	84:5	37:6	89:28	39:4	90:3
34:20	84:6	37:9	89:29	39:6	90:4
35:1	85:1	37:10	89:30	39:7	90:5
35:1	85:2	37:12	89:31	39:8	90:6
35:2	85:3	37:13	89:32	39:9	90:7

BATY	CHARLES	BATY	CHARLES	BATY	CHARLES
39:10	90:8	40:15	91:18	43:5	97:6
39:12	90:9	40:17	91:19	43:6	97:7
39:14	90:10	41:1	92:1	43:6	97:8
39:16	90:11	41:2	92:2	43:7	97:9
39:17	90:12	41:3	92:3	43:8	97:10
39:19	90:13	41:3	92:4	43:9	98:1
39:21	90:14	41:3	92:5	43:9	98:2
39:23	90:15	41:4	93:1	43:10	98:3
39:23	90:16	41:5	93:2	43:12	98:4
39:28	90:17	41:7	93:3	43:14	98:5
39:25	90:18	41:8	93:4	43:15	98:6
39:26	90:19	41:11	93:5	43:16	98:7
39:41	90:20	41:12	93:6	43:16	98:8
39:44	90:21	41:12	93:7	43:17	98:9
39:45	90:22	41:13	93:8	43:18	98:10
39:45	90:23	41:15	93:9	43:20	98:11
39:45	90:24	41:15	93:10	43:21	98:12
39:45	90:25	41:22	93:11	43:22	98:13
39:46	90:26	41:24	93:12	43:23	98:14
39:49	90:27	41:25	93:13	43:24	98:15
39:29	90:28	41:26	93:14	43:25	98:16
39:30	90:29	42:1	94:1	44:1	99:1
39:31	90:30	42:2	94:2	44:2	99:2
39:40	90:31	42:3	94:3	44:4	99:3
39:32	90:32	42:4	94:4	44:5	99:4
39:32	90:33	42:5	94:5	44:6	99:5
39:33	90:34	42:6	94:6	44:7	99:6
39:34	90:35	42:7	94:7	44:8	99:7
39:35	90:36	42:7	94:8	44:8	99:8
39:35	90:37	42:8	94:9	44:8	99:9
39:36	90:38	42:9	94:10	44:9	99:10
39:39	90:39	42:11	94:11	44:11	99:11
39:39	90:40	42:12	95:1	44:12	99:12
39:50	90:41	42:13	95:2	44:13	99:13
39:51	90:42	42:14	95:3	44:14	99:14
40:1	91:1	42:15	95:4	44:15	99:15
40:2	91:2	42:15	95:5	44:15	99:16
40:3	91:3	42:16	95:6	44:17	100:1
40:5	91:4	42:17	95:7	44:18	100:2
40:6	91:5	42:18	96:1	44:18	100:3
40:6	91:6	42:19	96:2	45:1	100:4
40:7	91:7	42:21	96:3	45:3	100:5
40:9	91:8	42:21	96:4	45:4	100:6
40:10	91:9	42:22	96:5	45:5	100:7
40:12	91:10	42:23	96:6	45:6	100:8
40:13	91:11	42:24	96:7	45:7	100:9
40:16	91:12	42:25	96:8	45:8	100:10
40:17	91:13	43:1	97:1	45:9	100:11
40:18	91:14	43:2	97:2	45:10	100:12
40:19	91:15	43:2	97:3	45:10	100:13
40:20	91:16	43:3	97:4	45:11	101:1
40:21	91:17	43:4	97:5	45:12	101:2

BATY	CHARLES	BATY	CHARLES
45:13	101:3	48:3	106:5
45:14	101:4	48:4	106:6
45:15	101:5	48:6	106:7
45:16	101:6	48:7	106:8
45:17	101:7	48:9	106:9
45:18	101:8	48:10	106:10
45:19	101:9	48:11	106:11
46:1	102:1	48:12	106:12
46:3	102:2	48:13	106:13
46:4	102:3	48:13	106:14
46:6	102:4	48:16	106:15
46:6	102:5	48:14	106:16
46:7	102:6	48:15	106:17
46:7	102:7	48:16	106:18
46:7	102:8	48:16	106:19
46:7	102:9	48:17	107:1
46:7	102:10	48:18	107:2
46:7	102:11	48:20	107:3
46:8	103:1	48:21	108:1
46:8	103:2	48:21	108:2
46:9	103:3	48:21	108:3
46:10	103:4	48:21	108:4
46:11	103:5	48:22	108:5
46:11	103:6	48:22	108:6
46:12	103:7	48:23	108:7
46:13	103:8	48:23	108:8
46:14	103:9	48:24	108:9
46:15	103:10	48:25	108:10
46:18	103:11	48:25	108:11
46:19	103:12	48:26	108:12
46:20	103:13	48:26	108:13
46:20	103:14	48:27	108:14
46:21	103:15	48:27	108:15
47:1	104:1	48:28	108:16
47:2	104:2		
47:2	104:3		
47:3	104:4		
47:3	104:5		
47:4	104:6		
47:5	104:7		
47:6	104:8		
47:6	104:9		
47:7	104:10		
47:9	104:11		
47:10	104:12		
47:11	104:13		
47:12	105:1		
47:13	105:2		
48:1	106:1		
48:2	106:2		
48:3	106:3		
48:3	106:4		

ISBN 978-168564450-5

Made in United States
North Haven, CT
28 May 2023

37076809R00114